I0455934

Me, Myself, and I

Unraveling the Mysteries of the
Mind and Self

By
Grant Mattos

To my wife Christina and daughter Flynn Parker Rose
without whom these words remain inside

Contents

The Journey Within

It starts inside. A curiosity. A whisper. It's more than the hum of daily routines, the clicking of keyboards, the clatter of commutes. It's a silence loud enough to make you listen. To turn your gaze inward. On the surface, we're professionals, navigating deadlines, meetings, that next promotion. But beneath the surface, there's a depth untold. This book is your invitation to dive.

Exploring the self isn't a task. It's a journey. No two paths the same. Not a straight line but a labyrinth. Full of corners, surprises. It's easy to get lost. Easier still to find yourself walking in circles. So why undertake such a journey? Because understanding the self is perhaps the most fundamental quest of our existence. It influences how we see the world, interact with others, make decisions. It shapes our perceptions, our realities.

Think of the mind as uncharted territory. Here we stand at the edge, peering into possibilities. What constructs our sense of self? Is it the roles we inhabit - professional, personal, social? Or something more

1

intrinsic, something carved into our very being? It's a question as old as time, threading through philosophy, psychology, spirituality.

The essence of self is not a textbook definition. You won't find it neatly outlined, bound by page numbers. It's a puzzle. Pieces scattered across the fields of our consciousness, waiting to be gathered. This book is not an answer. It's a guide. A way to navigate the journey within, to uncover the layers, to begin asking the questions that matter.

How do our brains weave the rich tapestry of self-awareness? From the synaptic dance that crafts our thoughts to the emotional undercurrents that color our experiences, our neurological landscape is vast, intricate. Yet, it's only one piece of the puzzle. Our minds, capable of such extraordinary feats, still bow to the mysteries of consciousness.

Psychology offers a lens, one way to view the spectrum of self. Behaviorism, cognitive theory, psychoanalytic perspectives - each provides keys, clues to understanding the cavernous spaces of our inner workings. But they, too, are just fragments of a much larger story.

Society, culture, language - they wrap around us, threads in the fabric of our being. How much of who we are is intrinsically us, and how much is woven by the world around us? The journey within delves into these layers, unraveling the tapestry, seeking the yarns of self untainted by external influence.

Emotions, those ephemeral tides, sway us. They are the music to which our lives dance, the palette from which our experiences are painted. Understanding this component of the self is akin to mastering the art of balance - allowing feelings to flow without letting them capsize the ship of our being.

Identity is not static. It is a series of masks, roles we slip into. The professional persona at work. The relational roles within families, friendships. Each mask, a facet of our inner diamond. But beneath these layers, is there an authentic self? A core untainted by expectation? The journey within seeks to polish the facets without losing sight of the gem.

Memory shapes us. It's the architect of our narrative, the scribe of our life's story. Yet, memory is fallible, malleable. It edits, erases, rewrites. How do we distinguish the essence of self amid this flux? How do we hold onto our core when the past is a shifting landscape?

Philosophy and spirituality offer bridges. Paths that cross the chasms of existential queries. "Who am I?" "Why am I here?" These questions are the compasses guiding our journey. Eastern wisdom,

Western thought, religious traditions, and the quiet introspection of meditation - they all beckon us deeper into the exploration of self.

The self is not a static entity; it's a river in constant flow. Life's transitions, the inevitable changes - they offer opportunities for reinvention, for resilience. The journey within is continuous, a spiraling closer to understanding, to acceptance, to growth.

And now, the digital age. Technology, with its virtual realities, its online personas, stretches the boundaries of self. It mirrors, distorts, amplifies. What does it mean to be oneself in a world where identity can be crafted, curated, and changed with clicks? The journey now spans new territories, uncharted cyber landscapes.

This book doesn't promise answers. It's not a map but a compass. It won't tell you who you are, but it will help you ask the right questions. Questions that lead not to destinations, but towards understanding, towards peace, towards a fuller embrace of the multitude within. The journey within is the bravest journey. It's time to begin.

So, as we turn these pages together, let's embark on this exploration of the self. With curiosity as our guide, let's unravel the conditioning, the constructs, the beautifully complex mosaic that is you. This journey is an invitation to discover not just who you are, but who you can become. Welcome to the journey within.

Chapter 1:
The Essence of Self:
Unveiling the Mystery

The essence of self remains an enigma, cloaked in the vast tapestry of existence. It's what you wake up to every morning, yet it hides beneath layers of routine, beneath the skin, reaching deeper into the marrow of existence than one often perceives. In-between the first sip of coffee and the last light of dusk, where does the 'I' reside? Philosophers, scientists, and sages have toiled to uncover this mystery, offering a plethora of perspectives that stretch across the horizon of thought. The self is not just an amalgam of random thoughts and fleeting emotions. It's a fortress built over years; its foundation lying in historical wisdom, its walls erected from the bricks of modern interpretation. But, within its core, the self is multifaceted—a triune entity comprising physical, mental, and spiritual dimensions. Each layer, an echo of our existence, calls for exploration beyond the superficial. It's in the understanding of this trinity that one can begin to unravel the threads that weave the intricate fabric of the 'self'. This chapter aims to cut through the layers, offering insights into these aspects, shedding light not just on what constitutes the self but also on the essence that is as eternal as it is elusive. Through the understanding of our physical being, the depths of our mental landscapes, and the heights of our spiritual quests, we embark on a journey to understand not just who we are, but what we are, in the grandest scheme of things.

What is the Self?

It starts with a whisper in the morning light, a question that threads through the rush of our daily lives, persisting, insistent. What, indeed, are we beyond the flesh and bone, beyond the roles we slip into as easily as our office attire? This self, it's a terrain we navigate from the moment consciousness flickers on, mapping its contours through the years. To say it's complex is an understatement; it's an ecosystem of memories, desires, beliefs, and so much more, evolving with every heartbeat. Traverse back through history, and you'll find a mosaic of interpretations, each culture and era sketching its outline of what makes us 'us.' Yet, here we stand, in the modern whirlwind, still grappling with the essence of our being. We seek in the mirror, in the quiet, for that unchanging core, wondering if it's merely a construct, shaped and reshaped by the endless stimuli or if, beneath the layers, there exists a singular, immutable self. This question isn't new. It's as old as time, yet it's ours now, to examine under the lens of our experiences, our struggles, our fleeting joys. As we delve into the depths, let's not search for concrete answers but embrace the journey itself, discovering along the way how our unique self is both the sculptor and the sculpture in the art of living.

Historical Perspectives

Time moves. It takes us from unknown pasts to uncertain futures. There's a thread in this movement. It's the self. Through history, this notion of self has been sculpted by philosophers, molded by religions, and analyzed by scientists. But let's rewind. Let's go back.

Imagine the ancients. The Greeks. Socrates pondering, "Know thyself." Simple words. Profound depths. This was more than advice. It was a command to delve into the psyche. The essence of self was not a topic left to the subconscious; it was central to understanding one's place in the universe.

Fast forward a few centuries. The East brings its own perspectives. In the sprawling lands of India, the Upanishads spoke of Atman, the soul, the self that is one with everything. Buddhism challenges this, promoting Anatta, or no-self, suggesting the idea of a permanent self is an illusion.

Move through time. The Enlightenment. Europe awakens. Descartes declares, "I think, therefore I am." With those words, the self took another turn. Identity became closely tied to cognition. To think was to be, and to be was to think. The self was rational, a clear and distinct idea.

Hume dissented. No core self, he argued, just a bundle of perceptions. What we call the "self" is nothing but a collection of fleeting moments stitched together by memory.

The industrial revolution uproots. Societies shift. The self becomes modern. Freud enters. The subconscious is unlocked. Dreams, desires, hidden in the depths of our psyche, dictate who we are. The self is no longer just a rational entity; it is driven by desires hidden beneath layers of consciousness.

Jung parts ways with Freud but explores deeper. Our personal unconscious is just the tip of the iceberg. Beneath lies the vast collective unconscious, shared across humanity. Archetypes, symbols, the Self – capital S – binding individuals to the collective story of humanity.

Across the ocean, William James brings pragmatism into play. The self is multifaceted: the social self, the material self, the spiritual self. Each influenced by the environment, each influencing how we interact with the world around us.

Mid-20th century, existentialism takes the stage. Sartre, Camus. The self is thrown into the world, responsible for defining itself. Essence follows existence. Our actions create our essence. The self is freedom, the self is anguish.

Simultaneously, the East gives us another lens. Lao Tzu, Chuang Tzu. Taoism emphasizes wu-wei, or effortless action. The self in harmony with the Tao acts naturally, effortlessly. The self is not separate from the world but a part of the ongoing flow of existence.

Fast forward again. Technology advances. The digital age. Our selves extend into virtual spaces. Online identities, social media personas. The self is no longer contained within the body or the mind; it proliferates across the digital universe.

Now, neuroscience steps in. The brain's plasticity highlights the self's fluidity. We are what we think, do, and experience. The self is malleable, constantly rewritten by our experiences. The past shapes us, but the future holds the power to redefine us.

In this whirlwind tour of historical perspectives, we've seen the self as rational and irrational, individual and collective, static and fluid. The journey through history is not just a study of ideas; it's an exploration of what it means to be human.

The self, then, is not a single entity but a kaleidoscope of perspectives, experiences, and theories. As we venture into modern interpretations, let's carry with us the wisdom of the past. The ancients pondered, the moderns analyzed, and we continue the quest, ever seeking to understand the essence of who we are.

So, we stand here. At the intersection of history and modernity. Looking back to see forward. The self, complex yet comprehensible, awaits our understanding. Let's move forward, armed with the knowledge that the quest to understand the self is as old as humanity itself, yet forever new.

Modern Interpretations

We live in a time where the self is both celebrated and scrutinized. It's a dance of identity in a digital age, under the microscope of social norms and the infinity of the internet. Modern interpretations of the self meander through complexities, threading ancient wisdom with the fabric of contemporary life.

What does it mean to "know thyself" in a world that constantly redefines the parameters of existence? The self, a concept as old as time, unwinds and rewinds, adapting to the tapestry of the now. Our ancestors pondered in caves; we ponder over screens. Yet, the quest remains unaltered. It's about peeling back layers. But today, the layers have new textures, vibrant and volatile, as we scroll and click through our existence.

Technological advancement brings about questions of authenticity. The digital self, an avatar of our choosing, frolics in the field of social media, sometimes disconnected from the flesh and blood reality. This schism, a hallmark of our era, beckons us to question the nature of our virtual presentations. Are they but mere veneers, or do they reveal deeper strata of our psyche?

A challenge emerges. To find equilibrium between the virtual and the visceral. It's a tightrope walk over the canyon of self-exploration. Mere existence in this dichotomy demands a degree of mindfulness previously unknown. We navigate these realms, crafting identities that ebb and flow with the tide of societal expectation and personal authenticity.

In the hustle of everyday life, the self is also a pocket of resistance. It's where we park our ideologies, our dreams, and our fears. It's more than just surviving; it's how we define living. And in the blur of routine, moments of silence anchor us back to the essence of our being.

The modern interpretation of the self is inherently plural. It is not one, but many. An amalgamation of roles, responsibilities, and realizations. We are multifaceted, and the acknowledgment of this multiplicity is both liberating and daunting. The self is no longer a static entity but a dynamic, evolving composition.

Mental health has taken center stage in our understanding of the self. It's a reflection of the mind's landscape, as crucial to our identity as the physical form. Societal stigma around mental health issues is challenged, unwound by the threads of open conversation and advocacy. Understanding ourselves includes confronting shadows, fears, biases. It's as much about healing as it is about growing.

The spiritual dimension, too, has seen a resurgence. It's not about religion per se, but about a search for meaning, for connection to something greater than the sum of our digital footprints. Meditation, mindfulness—these aren't just buzzwords but pathways to deeper introspection.

What of emotions in the modern frame? They are the colors with which we paint our self-portrait. Emotional intelligence is now recognized as a cornerstone of personal development. It's about navigating our internal landscapes with the grace of an experienced sailor, acknowledging storms, and appreciating calm seas alike.

Identity, a concept so bound up with the self, is now perceived as fluid. It's a spectrum, splashed across the canvas of humanity in all its vivid hues. Gender, sexuality, race, and beyond—the conversation has broadened, challenging us to envision identity as a broad landscape rather than a narrow corridor.

Changes in societal structure and expectations have a profound impact on our self-perception. The emergence of global consciousness invites us to reconsider our place in the world, not as isolated beings but as part of a complex ecosystem.

The role of memory in shaping our identity is underscored in the modern narrative. Personal narratives, constructed from the bricks of memory, contribute to our sense of continuity. Yet, in the digital age, with its relentless influx of information, the question of what we choose to remember and why becomes poignant.

Life transitions, once measured by predictable milestones, now occur in myriad forms. Each transition, whether chosen or thrust upon us, is an opportunity to renegotiate our understanding of self.

Adaptation and resilience, skills of survival, are heralds of personal evolution.

As we seek to redefine purpose and meaning in a rapidly changing world, existential questions linger. They hover at the edges of our consciousness, whispering of potential, of possibility. "Who am I?" remains a query as relevant today as it was millennia ago. But now, it's asked in a world where the self can be both a construct and a deeply felt essence.

And so, modern interpretations of the self are a kaleidoscope, ever-shifting, reflecting the complexity of contemporary life. They urge us to consider the multiplicity within, to embrace the multitude of selves we host. It's a journey inward, as ancient as it is urgent, beckoning us toward a profound engagement with the essence of who we are, in the here and now.

The Multifaceted Nature of the Self

We're more than what we see, feel, and think. This truth, simple yet profound, escapes us in the rush of the everyday. Our self is not a monolith; it's multifaceted, a prism splitting light into various colors. Imagine, if you will, the physical self, the vessel that carries us through the world. It's tangible, visible, often obsessively groomed or critiqued. But it's just one aspect. The mental self, a labyrinth of thoughts, beliefs, dreams, often running like a river, sometimes calm, sometimes raging. We're sculpted by these currents, yet not solely defined by them. Then there's the spiritual self, perhaps the most elusive. A quiet whisper in a noisy room, suggesting that we're part of something larger, interconnected in ways that defy easy explanation. This triad—physical, mental, spiritual— shapes our existence, each aspect influencing the others in an intricate dance. Understanding this trifecta doesn't simplify us; rather, it opens up the complexity and richness of what it means to be human. As we peel back layers, uncover the conditioning, we start to see the self in its true form: boundless, evolving, a mystery beckoning us closer.

Physical Self

It's the body. It's what you see in the mirror every morning. Or what you avoid seeing. It's what you feel when you're too tired to climb another stair or too energized to sleep. The physical self is tangible, the most evident aspect of our being, yet often, it's the most overlooked, taken for granted until it signals, sometimes loudly, that it needs attention.

We exist in a world where mind and matter are intricately connected. The physical self isn't just a vessel. It's a library of experiences, a repository of energy, a testament to existence. How we treat it, how we respect it, tells a story not just to the world but to our inner selves about who we are, what we value.

To understand the physical self is to recognize its impact on every other aspect of our being. It's more than muscle, bone, and skin. It's the interface through which we interact with reality, a medium of expression, of pain, joy, and the mundane. Health isn't just absence of illness. It's vitality, it's the capacity to engage fully with life.

The physical self evolves, grows from infancy through the turbulence of adolescence, into the steadiness or sometimes unsteadiness of adulthood, and into the wisdom of old age. This journey isn't just marked by physical milestones but by the memories etched into our very cells.

Movement and stillness, both define the physical self. The rush of adrenaline and the calm of a deep breath. They coexist, shaping our responses, influencing our choices, our interactions. Exercise, then, becomes not just a routine for physical health but a practice of mindfulness, a tuning into the rhythm of life.

Nutrition plays a role not just in sustaining the body but in nourishing the soul. Food, in its essence, is energy. It's information. What we consume communicates with our cells, influences our mood, our energy levels, our capacity to think clearly. Eating, thus, becomes an act of mindfulness, a choice that echoes across the dimensions of self.

Rest, often underrated, is profound. Sleep, a surrender to the night, a trust in the body's wisdom to heal, to rejuvenate. In stillness, growth. In rest, the consolidation of learning, the processing of experiences. It's as vital as air, yet we often starve ourselves of it amidst the hustle of proving worth.

Then there's touch, an elemental need. Skin hunger, they call it. The physical self longs for connection, not just in the metaphorical heart but in the literal, tactile sense. A hug, a handshake, a pat on the back, these are not just social niceties but nutritional needs for the physical self, speaking in the language of connection, belonging.

Appearance, the mirror's tale. It's complicated. The reflection stares back, sometimes a friend, often a critic. It's not vanity to care for it but respect, an acknowledgement of the self's worth. Yet, it's a slippery slope where societal expectations shadow personal well-being.

The physical self, it ages. Wrinkles, greying hair, the slowing down. Society tells a story of decline, but there's another narrative — one of grace, of accumulated wisdom, of a body that has lived, laughed, and endured. Aging is not just a biological process but a cultural construct, ripe for redefinition.

Illness, when it comes, is a dialogue. Sometimes a confrontation, a renegotiation of existence. It's not just a physical ordeal but a mental, emotional, spiritual journey. Healing, then, is holistic, a path through the physical self to the very core of being.

Sexuality, an integral part of the physical self, is more than biological. It's an avenue of expression, intimacy, creativity. It bridges the self to another, not just in physicality but through the layers of emotion, vulnerability, and sometimes, transformation.

The physical self in silence. Meditation, yoga, the still practices—they tune the body, quiet the mind, knit the fragments of self into wholeness. In stillness, we find not just the strength but the flexibility, not just the boundary but the bridge.

Ultimately, the physical self is the starting point, the journey, and in many ways, the destination. It's the dimension of self that we navigate the world with, the aspect of being that we interact with reality through. To nurture it is not just an act of self-care but an act of radical acceptance, a profound saying 'yes' to existence.

So, we tend to it, listen, care, for in its vitality, resilience, and yes, even its vulnerability, we find not just health but meaning, connection, the very essence of life itself. The physical self, in all its tangible reality, is a narrative we live, a story we tell, not just with words but with every breath, every step, every heartbeat.

Mental Self

It's a vast sea. Dark and deep. Full of promise and peril. We navigate its waters daily, often without thought, setting sails on vessels built from habits and thoughts long ingrained.

We are our thoughts. They say. But who shapes these thoughts? From the crisp edge of consciousness, a thought emerges. Uninvited. It weaves into the fabric of our being, sometimes nestling comfortably, sometimes sticking out, a splinter in the mind.

Mornings are crisp. We awaken, not just from sleep but from a suspension of the self. The mental self stirs, stretching into the spaces of the waking world. It picks up where it left off, continuing the narrative, the inner monologue that had paused for rest.

Work demands attention. Sharp. Focused. The mental self shifts, adapting to the role required. It's malleable, able to don the professional mask. Yet, beneath the surface, the undercurrents of personal identity and doubt swirl. Ever-present. Ever-persistent.

Interactions are transactions. Each exchange subtly shapes our mental self. It's an economy of influence.

We give. We take. Each word, each look, each dismissal, a currency contributing to our evolving sense of self. Impactful yet unnoticed.

Time alone is rare. In solitude, the mental self speaks loudest. It questions. It doubts. It affirms. It's in these quiet moments that the foundation shakes, and from these tremors, new understandings can emerge. Transformation begins in stillness.

The past is a shadow. Memories shape us but can also ensnare us. The mental self clings to these shadows, sometimes finding comfort, other times, chains. Unlocking these chains requires facing the shadows, understanding them, and ultimately, stepping into the light.

We are creatures of habit. Daily rituals shape the mental self, carving pathways through the dense jungle of our minds. These paths can lead to enlightenment or entrapment. The choice of route, consciously chosen or unwittingly wandered upon, determines the destination.

Emotional turmoil is a storm. Thoughts become turbulent waves crashing against the fragile barriers we erect. The mental self can be the lighthouse, guiding us through the storm, or it can be the tempest, tearing down our defenses.

Choices define us. Every decision, every path taken, contributes to the narrative of the self. The mental self is the author of this story, yet it often feels penned by an unseen hand. The struggle for authorship is constant and consuming.

Beliefs anchor us. They provide stability in an ever-changing sea of information and influence. But these anchors can also hold us back, preventing exploration and growth. The mental self must weigh these anchors, deciding which to hoist and which to let sink.

Knowledge is power. It lights the way, revealing paths previously hidden. The mental self seeks knowledge, craves it, but must also question it. For in questioning, we find deeper truths, and with each truth, the self evolves.

Connections are lifelines. The mental self does not exist in isolation. It's shaped by every interaction, every relationship. These connections can nourish the self, providing sustenance for growth, or they can drain, leaving the self diminished.

Change is inevitable. The mental self of today will not be the same tomorrow. It's a constant metamorphosis, influenced by experiences, shaped by decisions, and refined by time. Embracing this change is embracing the self in its entirety.

Understanding the mental self is the journey of a lifetime. It's a voyage into the depths of our being, exploring unknown territories, confronting monsters, and discovering treasures. It requires courage, curiosity, and compassion. For in understanding the mental self, we unlock the full potential of our humanity.

Spiritual Self

It's quiet here. In the realm of the spiritual self, words lose their heft. Actions carry weight, sure. But intentions? They're the currency. The working professional knows this. Day in. Day out. Actions colored by intention.

Some find it in faith. In the hush of prayer or the chant of meditation. A mosque. A church. A temple. Nature. Places sanctified by sincerity, not just bricks and mortar. The spiritual self is about connection. Not just to a higher power but to the world. To people.

Values. They guide us. More than profit margins and KPIs. Values rooted in the spiritual self steer actions. Integrity. Compassion. Empathy. Values that don't just dictate what we do but who we are. Who we become.

Lessons come. Sometimes in success. Other times, failure. The spiritual self sees both as teachers. Growth.

Evolution. Not confined to the corporeal, the career ladder. But inner growth. The kind that leaves us different. Changed.

It's a quest. The spiritual self's journey. One not marked by milestones of the conventional sort. But by moments. Moments of insight. Of peace. Of realization. Moments that, when pieced together, form the tapestry of our spiritual being.

In silence, we find it. The essence of the spiritual self. In those moments when the noise fades, and we are left with our thoughts. Our beliefs. Our essence. That's where discovery happens. In the silence.

Endings lead to beginnings. The spiritual self understands this. Embraces it. Every ending, an opportunity for a new beginning. A chance to reconsider. To reevaluate. To renew. The cyclical nature of life, mirrored in the spiritual journey.

Chapter 2:
The Birth of Consciousness

Imagine, for a moment, a void. Not the absence of light, but the absence of awareness. From this emptiness, consciousness emerges—faint at first, like the distant stars at dawn, then growing brighter, more insistent. It's a journey from the unfathomable depths of nothingness to the sparkling surface of awareness. What triggers this awakening? It begins in the silence, in the spaces between thoughts, where the mind whispers secrets to itself. Consciousness is born of complexity, of the brain's intricate dance. It's a process as mysterious as it is fundamental, illuminating the self from within like a lantern in the dark. This luminescence, this consciousness, is what distinguishes existence from living. But how does the brain, a tangled web of neurons and electrical impulses, give rise to this profound awareness? It's a question that occupies the space between science and philosophy, a bridge built from questions, leading us towards understanding. Yet, as we traverse this bridge, we realize that the birth of consciousness is not just a moment in time but a continuous unfolding, a story that each of us writes with every thought, every sensation, every breath. It's a journey through the self, within the self, a quest not just for awareness, but for understanding.

From Nothingness to Awareness

In the quiet before existence, there was nothing. In that nothing, a spark ignited, blossoming into awareness. This is not just a tale from ancient philosophies, but a mirrored story of each consciousness.

The birth of consciousness is subtle, almost imperceptible. It doesn't announce itself; it simply begins. Like the softest whisper of wind, it stirs the leaves of existence, barely detectable. Yet, this quiet beginning marks the genesis of self.

This transition is monumental, yet often overlooked. It's a journey from absolute darkness to the first breaking light of dawn. It's the first sense of 'I am' that whispers in the mind of the newborn, the initial realization of existence.

Consider the moment a child first recognizes themselves in a mirror. This moment is a milestone in the understanding of self. It's not merely visual recognition but an awakening. A realization of 'That's me.' From such moments, awareness spirals outward.

It's tempting to think of awareness as a switch that flicks on. In reality, it's more a gradual illumination. It's nurtured by interactions, shaped by experiences, and refined by the passage of time.

This journey is deeply personal, yet universally shared. It connects every conscious being. In this light, we see not just the self but the reflection of all life's complexity mirrored back.

And so, from nothingness, awareness blooms. It's a profound transformation that sets the stage for all that follows. The journey of self-awareness that begins in the silence of non-existence is the canvas upon which the story of life is drawn.

The Role of the Brain in Self-Awareness

The brain navigates us through an ocean of sensory information, sifting, sorting, rejecting, and embracing. It sculpts our reality. What we perceive as the self emerges from this relentless processing. It's the brain's selective attention to certain stimuli and its disregard for others that constructs the narrative of who we are.

Neurons communicate in whispers and shouts. Signals cascade like waterfalls, each drop a piece of information. This is the language of the brain, the underpinning of our consciousness. Our thoughts, memories, feelings - they're all etched into these biological currents.

We take it for granted, this sense of "I." Yet, it's the outcome of billions of neurons firing and wiring together, a symphony orchestrated by the brain's relentless activity. The self is a construct, a narrative pieced together from the fabric of experience, all processed and stored within the brain.

Consider moments of deep reflection. The brain scans through memories, beliefs, desires, weaving them into the tapestry of our identity. This introspection is the brain's way of updating the narrative of the self, refining it with each new experience.

There's a raw beauty in the brain's complexity. Its capacity to give rise to consciousness, to self-awareness, is one of evolution's most mysterious gifts. It's a puzzle we're only beginning to decipher. Each discovery peels back a layer, revealing not just how we become aware of ourselves but how we navigate the vastness of the human experience.

The brain is not just an organ of thought but of feeling. Emotions color our self-awareness, adding depth and texture to our sense of identity. The brain interprets these emotions, integrating them into our self-narrative. This interplay between thought and feeling is at the heart of self-awareness.

In the end, the journey into consciousness is a journey into the brain. Its structures and functions, its capabilities and limitations, shape our awareness of the self. Understanding the role of the brain in self-awareness is not just an academic pursuit. It's a key to unlocking the mysteries of who we are and how we fit into the world around us.

Chapter 3:
The Neurological Self

In the depths of the mind, where thought merges with existence, lies the neurological self. It's a realm where neurons communicate in whispers and shouts, forming the tapestry of our consciousness. Here, the brain isn't just an organ; it's the architect of our reality. Neuroplasticity reveals to us that our experiences, both mundane and profound, are carpenters of this architecture. The brain shapes and is shaped in return, a dialogue between the world and the self. Consider the limbic system, the seat of our emotions; it colors our perceptions, dictates our reactions. Love, fear, joy, despair; they're not just feelings but neurochemical symphonies. And when disorder enters this delicate system, the self may feel like a stranger in one's own mind. Yet, understanding the brain's role in making us who we are brings a sense of liberation. We are not fixed beings but works in progress, continuously sculpted by the intricate dance of neurons. In grasping the neurological self, we edge closer to the heart of the mystery: What makes 'me' me?

Understanding the Brain's Role

The saga of comprehension winds through the labyrinths of our brains, where every corner turned unveils more about our selves. It's there, in the deep recesses of our neurological landscapes, that our identity dances with the synaptic pulses firing ceaselessly. We've wandered through the chapters, seen the self from myriad angles, but it's here, pondering the brain's role, that the convergence of our quest lies. Brains, marvelous in their complexity, house the essence of our thoughts, feelings, and the very conception of who we are. This flesh-bound processor doesn't just manage our bodily functions; no, it's an orchestra, conducting the symphony of our consciousness. The brain shapes us, molds our perceptions, and colors our realities with a palette known only to itself. Like clay, our neural pathways are etched with experiences, reconfigured by our interactions, and constantly rewritten by the stories we tell ourselves. We dive into the brain not as a mechanic seeking to dismantle, but as explorers, yearning to understand the fabric of our being. In this voyage, we uncover the mysteries not just of the self, but of the neurological self, woven intricately within the folds of our cerebrum.

Neuroplasticity and Identity

Flow from the last chapter into this, it's clear the brain's not just sitting up there. It's changing.

Imagine a river, carving canyons through rock. Not overnight. Over millennia. That's neuroplasticity. But quicker. Our experiences, thoughts, the very essence of our lives reshaping our brains. And so, our identities.

Think, for a moment, who you were ten years ago. Not the same person reading this, I bet. Changed jobs, perhaps. Made new friends, lost others. Loved, maybe lost. Each experience a raindrop in the river, altering the landscape of your mind.

It's personal, but it's science too. Every new skill, every habit formed, your brain's working behind the scenes. Neurons firing together, wiring together. And just like that, you're playing the piano, or you've quit smoking. Your brain's changed. You've changed.

But it's a double-edged sword, isn't it? Neuroplasticity doesn't discern between the good and the bad. Stress, anxiety, that too carves deep channels. Over time, our reactions, our very personality can shift. Sometimes so gradually, we don't even notice it's happening.

Questions arise, then. If our brains, and so our identities, are in constant flux, who are we really? Are we merely the sum of our experiences, or is there something more innate to our sense of self?

This is where we tread carefully, delicately balancing on the edge of philosophy and neuroscience. Our identities aren't just what we do, or think, or feel. They're deeply influenced by the plasticity of our brains, yes, but there's resilience there too. A core self, perhaps.

Consider resilience. Life's inevitable hardships can reshape us, often in profound ways. Yet, many find a way back, or to a new version of themselves. If our brains were simply malleable clay without any inherent form, could such resilience exist? Doubtful.

And here's where it gets fascinating. Our conscious efforts to change can harness neuroplasticity in our favor. Think mindfulness, meditation, cognitive behavioral therapy. These aren't just good habits. They're tools, powerful tools, for self-directed brain remodeling.

But pause for a moment. If we can, to some extent, direct our brain's plasticity, choose who we become, doesn't that place a tremendous responsibility on our shoulders? It does. It means our actions, our thoughts, even our environment, are part of this ongoing construction project that is our self.

Yet, how freeing is that thought? Not slaves to our biology, nor to our past, but sculptors of our future selves. With knowledge, with effort, we can perhaps become who we aspire to be.

But, and there's always a but, change is hard. It's slow. It's often two steps forward, one step back. The river doesn't carve through the rock overnight. Patience, then, patience and persistence, are key.

We circle back, then, to identity. It's not static, never was. Shaped by the plastic mind, yes, but also shaping that very mind. A feedback loop, of sorts. We are both the sculptor and the marble, the river and the canyon.

In the end, this recognition of our brain's plasticity, its intimate connection to our sense of self, is not just academic. It's deeply personal, profoundly empowering. To know that we have the capacity for change, that our identity is a dynamic interplay of biology, experience, and will, is to hold the key to the art of becoming.

The Limbic System and Emotions

In the depths of the brain, where secrets hide and truths wait to be uncovered, lies the limbic system. It's more than just a center; it's a world of emotional complexity, guiding much of what we feel and, by extension, who we are.

Sit still for a moment. Let thoughts come and go. It's here, in this quiet space, you might sense the undercurrents of emotions that often guide actions unseen. The limbic system works beneath consciousness, a silent influencer of sorts.

Understanding this, one steps into an arena where emotions and the self are entwined in an intricate dance. To understand the self, one must first grapple with this system's role. It's a journey into the unseen facets of our being.

The brain is a marvel, and at its emotional core lies the limbic system. Think of it as an orchestra conductor, directing the flow of emotional responses and coloring every experience with emotional hues.

In the vastness of our brain, structures like the hippocampus, amygdala, and hypothalamus play leading roles. The amygdala, for instance, orchestrates our responses to fear, sculpting memories with emotional weight, training the mind to remember what to embrace and what to avoid.

Life's moments are tinted with emotions, a palette vast and intricate. These colors stem from the limbic system, mixing and melding within the canvas of our consciousness.

Walk through a busy street. Every face you see, every interaction, sparks a myriad of emotional responses, subtle yet significant. This is the limbic system at work, navigating the complex web of human emotions and societal norms.

In moments of solitude, when the mind wanders to places both deep and dark, or light and hopeful, the limbic system crafts these experiences. Emotions guide thoughts, and thoughts, in turn, fuel emotions, a cycle of influence that shapes the psyche.

Consider for a moment the power of emotion in memory. A scent, a song, a scene glimpsed briefly through a window - each can evoke powerful, visceral memories. This bond between memory and emotion, forged in the limbic system, underpins our very sense of self.

It's in the subtleties of these experiences that we find the shades of our emotional selves. What makes one's heart swell in joy or shrink in sorrow is deeply personal, yet universally understood through the language of the limbic system.

The dance of emotions isn't one of mere chance. It's choreographed by evolutionary necessity, a guide to survival in a world where feeling can dictate the difference between safety and peril.

Within the professional realm, where logic often reigns supreme, emotions carve out their own space. Decision-making, leadership, empathy, and interpersonal dynamics are all suffused with the invisible hand of the limbic system.

To traverse this landscape of emotions, one must embark on a journey of self-exploration. Turning inward, we encounter our limbic selves, a territory rich with the nuances of joy, fear, love, and despair.

This inward journey reveals not just the origins of our emotional responses but also the conditioning of our minds. The recognition that emotions are both a response to the external world and a construct of our internal dialogues opens avenues for understanding, growth, and ultimately, transformation.

Thus, the limbic system stands not just as a relic of our evolutionary past but as a beacon for self-discovery. In its depths lie the keys to unraveling the intricate tapestry of the self, a journey that, while deeply personal, resonates with the universal quest for understanding the essence of who we are.

Brain Disorders and the Sense of Self

It's like we're on a road. Days stretch out. Life rolls on. But for some, an unexpected turn. A brain disorder sweeps in, and the sense of self, that solid ground, shifts. We dive deep here, exploring this less trodden path. Here's where the fabric frays, and the intimate dance between the neurological and the personal reveals its complex patterns.

Beyond the veil of common experience, brain disorders beckon us with a stark reminder: the self is not a constant. Conditions such as Alzheimer's and schizophrenia don't just affect the brain; they unravel the self. They whisper to us of a self that is more fragile, more intertwined with the neurological than we'd like to admit. Yet, in these whispers, there's a depth of understanding waiting to be uncovered.

The self, after all, isn't merely built. It's woven, thread by thread, by memories, thoughts, feelings. Imagine, then, the fabric tearing. Alzheimer's, a thief in the night, steals memories. What happens to the self when the threads run thin? It shifts, changes, sometimes becoming unrecognizable even to those closest. The person who once was—is no longer. Or, at least, not in the way they used to be.

Then there's schizophrenia, painting the world in different hues. Voices, unseen yet heard. Realities, vivid yet constructed. For those looking in, it's a window cracked. But for the one living it, it's a reality as real as any. Their sense of self adheres not to the world most know, but to the one their brain conjures.

It's a stark reminder—our selves are crafted not just socially, but neurologically.

And what of lesser-known conditions? Phantom limb syndrome, where a missing limb is felt so vividly. The brain insists, the self believes—it's there. This, too, tells a tale. Our physical self, it seems, is not just the body we see but the body the brain believes in. The self becomes a battleground, the known pitted against the known-to-be-true.

In diving into these conditions, there's a temptation to seek only the loss, the disintegration of the self. But there's more to be found. Consider epilepsy, where seizures can thrust one into an altered state of consciousness. Here, some find a profound alteration in their sense of self, a transcendent experience. It's a reminder that even in disorder, the self can touch new terrains, can expand beyond borders previously known.

The brain, in its complexity, holds not just the keys to disorders but the foundations of the self. In mapping these conditions—these deviations from the neurological norm—we uncover pieces of the puzzle. Pieces that tell us the self is not just a social construct or a narrative spun. It is, deeply, neurologically rooted.

Every thought we cherish, every memory we hold dear, sits within this neurological framework. When the framework falters, so does the narrative. The self can become disjointed, fragmented. Yet, it's in this fragmentation that a truth emerges: the self is malleable, adaptable, resilient. Even in the face of disorder, it seeks coherence, continuity.

Take amnesia. Here, the past slips away, and with it, the anchor of many a self. Yet, people adapt, create new anchors, new selves from the fragments left. It speaks to a self that's not just rooted in past experience, but capable of regeneration, of birthing anew amidst the ruins.

A question then, perhaps unanswerable: If our neurology changes—through disorder or otherwise—do we become someone new? Or do we remain, at our core, the same? It's a philosophical quandary, rooted in the churnings of the brain.

This exploration, it winds and weaves through the neurological landscape, uncovering the myriad ways in which brain disorders affect the sense of self. And yet, it's not just a journey into loss or change. It's a testament to resilience, to the unyielding nature of the self, even in the face of profound neurological storms.

In this realm where brain and self intertwine, there's an unspoken dialogue, a continuous exchange. Disorders disrupt, displace, disorient. But they also teach, reveal, illuminate. They show us the self in all its fragility, yes. But also its strength, its adaptability, its unfathomable depth.

So we journey, through the landscape of the neurological self, with an eye not just to the disorders that challenge it, but to the insights they offer. In the unraveling, we find threads of a deeper understanding of what it means to be. The self, ever-evolving, shaped by forces both within and beyond, stands as a testament to the intricate dance between the brain and the myriad elements that constitute our being.

In this, there's a reflection of the broader human condition. Each of us, navigating our own paths, faces shifts in our sense of self. They may not always stem from brain disorders, but the essence of the transformation resonates. It's in the ebb and flow of our neurological landscapes that we find the contours of our selves, continuously sculpted, endlessly emerging.

Thus, we circle back. To the road. To the journey. With each step, each turn, our understanding deepens. The self, with all its complexities, emerges not just as a construct of mind, but as a living, breathing entity, shaped in the crucible of our brains. Here, amidst the struggle and the strife, lies the beauty of becoming, of the endless unfolding of the self.

Chapter 4:
Psychological Perspectives
on the Self

The path we've tread so far wades deeper, crossing into the realm where psychology lays its foundations on understanding the self. Behavioral patterns write stories in the sands of our subconscious, each step a testament to the framework of behaviorism shaping who we are, what we do. And yet, cognition, the way we perceive, think, remember, intertwines with our very concept of self, crafting it with the finesse of an artist's brush. Within this twisted vine, the psychoanalytic perspective burrows, uncovering the layers beneath, peeling back the facade to reveal the inner workings, the quiet whispers of our deeper selves. This chapter navigates through these roads, forks in the psychological path that lead to our current understanding of self. It's more than just the brain, more than neurons firing patterns in the dark. It's the intricate dance of thoughts, behaviors, and hidden drives that constructs the mirror through which we see ourselves. In dissecting these perspectives, we inch closer to the core, closer to the illumination of our own minds' conditioning, peering into the abyss, not with trepidation but with the keen eye of an explorer, seeking truth in the psychological underbrush.

Behaviorism and the Self

Imagine stepping into the daylight, mind clear, the world anew. The sunlight hits your face and in that moment, you're nothing and everything all at once. B. F. Skinner stood in this philosophical arena, arguing not for the unseen self but for behavior as the end all. The self, then, a sum of observable actions, nothing hidden, nothing mystic.

The road is less traveled here. This simplistic view, free of the clutter of inner thoughts, dives into the essence of behaviorism. The self doesn't hide in shadowed thoughts or unspoken dreams but in the light of day, in actions taken, in words spoken. What you do is who you are. Simplistic, yes, but therein lies its beauty.

Skinner tossed the coin of free will and found it wanting. Everything we are, every piece of the self, conditioned by our environment. The clank of the coin, the reinforcement, the punishment - shaping us, molding the self as clay.

But what of spontaneity? The sudden laugh, the leap into the unknown. Do these not speak of a self unconditioned, a self free? Skinner would argue these are but illusions, the unpredictability of a complex system. We remain, in his eyes, predictable.

In the heart of behaviorism, we find reinforcement - the lynchpin. The child learns to speak, to walk, to act under the unseen hand of reinforcement. What's rewarded is repeated, shaping the burgeoning self into a societal fit.

Consider the power of this perspective. The self, malleable, ever-changing, shaped not from within but from without. No longer are we prisoners of an innate self but architects of change. This is the power Skinner hands us, the power of adaptation, of transformation.

Yet, the whisper of doubt creeps in. Is there not more? The internal dialogue, the dreams that shape our aspirations, the fears that haunt our steps. Can behaviorism's lens capture the full spectrum of the self?

The complexity of the human condition often escapes simple explanations. Skinner's realm is behavior, observable, measurable. But beneath this simplicity lies an undercurrent of complexity. Behavior matters, indeed, but so do the silent whispers of thought, the quiet dreams, the inner turmoil.

Life is an interplay of external pressures and inner drives. The workplace shapes us, yes, but so do our aspirations. We learn not just to adapt but to imagine, to create. The self is not just made in the image of the world but also molds the world in its image.

Behaviorism serves as a mirror, reflecting the power of the environment on the self. Yet, this reflection captures only part of the scene. The self, peering into the mirror, wonders about what lies beyond its edge. The thoughts unobservable, the dreams unmeasurable, they too shape the self.

The dialogue between behaviorism and the self is ongoing. Skinner's legacy, powerful, undeniable, lays the groundwork. It reminds us of the power of our actions, the strength of our environment. Yet, it also invites us to question, to explore beyond its boundaries.

In the dance of existence, our steps are shaped by both the seen and the unseen. The behaviorist's path, clear, defined, is but one route through the labyrinth of self. It awards us clarity, simplicity, a map of sorts. But as with any map, its edges are finite, its depiction incomplete.

As working professionals, we navigate this world, influenced by Skinner's insights. We adapt, we learn, we shape and are shaped. Yet, we also reach beyond, fueled by the unseen drives, the unmeasurable dreams. The self, in its entirety, is both the dancer and the dance, shaped by behavior, but also shaping itself through the unseen, the unspoken, the profound.

In embracing behaviorism, we grasp a tool, a perspective. But in recognizing its limits, we open the door to the vast landscape of the self. A landscape where actions speak, yes, but where the whispers of the self guide us through the unseen paths of existence.

The journey within, then, is not a straight path but a winding road, lit by behaviorism, but also shadowed by the complexities of the self. In this journey, we are both observers and participants, shaped by the world and shaping it in return. The self, in its quest for understanding, traverses both the observable and the unobservable, in a never-ending quest for understanding.

Cognitive Psychology and Self-Concept

Waves crash. Minds wander. The self seems a shore, both defined and sifted by thought's relentless tide. Cognitive psychology guides us through the labyrinth of the self-concept. It holds a mirror to our mind, asking not only who we are but how we come to know this self.

The mind, a fertile ground for the seeds of self-concept, sprouts belief and identity. Through childhood, we're painters, strokes broad and unsure. With time, the strokes become precise, our self-portrait growing clearer. Cognitive psychology suggests this clarity emerges from our interactions, thoughts filtering through experiences like sunlight through leaves.

Consider memory. It's like an old, dusty bookshelf, cluttered yet cherished. Each memory, a tome of our existence, contributes to the grand narrative of who we believe we are. Cognitive psychology posits that our self-concept is this library, constantly rewritten and revised by new experiences and insights.

And yet, biases cloud our self-perception. We are the heroes in our own stories, often blind to the plot twists and turns that challenge our sense of self. Cognitive dissonance, that uncomfortable clash between what we believe and what is, forces us to edit our narrative, to reconcile or reshape our self-concept.

Labels stick. They're like the names we give to storms, making them easier to categorize but not to understand. Cognitive psychology unpacks the labels we affix to ourselves and others, revealing how these identifiers can limit or liberate our self-perception.

Language, the tool of our thoughts, shapes our reality. It's both a bridge and a barrier to understanding our self-concept. How we talk about ourselves, to ourselves, molds our identity, cementing or chiseling away at the bedrock of our being.

Decisions, the crossroads of cognition, reflect and shape our self-concept. Each choice is a brick in the edifice of identity. Cognitive psychology explores this interplay, illustrating how the paths we choose both reveal and determine who we are.

Errors in our thought process, those moments we falter, illuminate the contours of our self-concept. Mistakes, far from mere missteps, are guideposts signaling the gaps in our understanding of ourselves.

The self is not static. It's dynamic, an ever-evolving narrative crafted by cognition. Our self-concept expands with each new chapter of life, each experience casting a stone into the mosaic of our identity.

Empathy, understanding another's thoughts and feelings, mirrors back our own identity. In grasping the mind of another, we navigate the depths of our own self-concept, discovering undiscovered shores within ourselves.

Goals, those distant lighthouses guiding our journey, illuminate the edges of our self-concept. In striving, in reaching, we sketch the outer bounds of who we are and who we might become.

Fears and flaws, though often shunned, are the dark matter of our self-concept. They shape us in their avoidance, drawing the map of our limitations and potentials in shadow.

Judgment, internal and external, etches its lines into our self-concept. Through the scrutiny of others and ourselves, we refine our identity, sanding down rough edges in the pursuit of some semblance of self.

The journey within, a trek through the terrain of thoughts and beliefs, leads us to the heart of our self-concept. Cognitive psychology offers the compass for this expedition, charting the course through the mind's mists.

In understanding the dance of cognition and self-concept, we embrace the multitude within. The self, a constellation of thoughts, memories, and beliefs, shines brighter with the light of awareness. And in this light, we find not just the self but the path to becoming who we wish to be.

Psychoanalytic Views on the Inner Self

The mind is a deep, sometimes dark, ocean. Its depths unexplored, its mysteries veiled in shadow. There's more to us than meets the eye, beneath the surface of conscious thoughts and actions. This is the realm of psychoanalysis—the domain of the inner self. A place Freud famously navigated with his metaphorical lantern, shedding light on our most hidden corners.

At the heart of psychoanalytic theory lies a simple, yet profound idea: we are not masters in our own house. The decisions we think we make, the desires we believe are ours, often stem from a place within us that we rarely visit consciously. Our inner self is a storehouse of feelings, memories, and wishes, many of which we've pushed away, deemed unacceptable or too painful to face.

Consider the mind an iceberg. What you see on the surface, the conscious mind, is only a fraction. Below lies the vastness of the unconscious, the true driver of the ship. Here dwell the thoughts and feelings we're not aware of, yet they guide much of our behavior. This unseen force shapes our perceptions, judgments, and interactions with the world and ourselves.

Freud introduced the idea of the id, ego, and superego. Three entities in a perpetual dance within our psyche. The id, driven by basic impulses for pleasure and aggression. The ego, the mediator, grounded in reality, striving to fulfill the id's desires in acceptable ways. The superego, our moral compass, often at odds with the id, instilling feelings of guilt and pride. This trinity composes our internal world, each part influencing our sense of self.

One can't discuss psychoanalysis without delving into the past. It asserts that our childhood experiences mold us, shape the adults we become. The relationships we had, the emotions we felt, the environments we navigated. These early interactions lay the foundation of our inner self, planting seeds that grow into the complexities of our adult personality.

Defense mechanisms are our mind's bodyguards. When internal conflicts arise, when the ego feels threatened, these mechanisms kick into high gear, protecting us from distress. Denial, repression, projection, these are but a few tools in our psychological arsenal, employed to keep uncomfortable truths at bay. Yet, they also keep us from fully understanding ourselves.

Psychoanalysis invites us to lie on the proverbial couch and look within. To ask why we feel what we feel, why we do what we do. It's not an easy journey. It requires us to confront parts of ourselves we've kept hidden. But it's in this exploration, in this brave act of self-reflection, that we can find freedom.

Our dreams, according to psychoanalytic thought, are gateways to the unconscious. Nightly, in the theatre of our minds, our deepest desires, fears, and conflicts are played out. Freud called dreams "the royal road to the unconscious," a path leading straight to the core of our inner self. By interpreting our dreams, we can uncover truths about ourselves that we've ignored or suppressed.

Then there's the concept of transference. In therapy, the feelings and expectations we unconsciously hold towards important figures from our past are transferred onto the therapist. This can be a powerful tool, allowing us to uncover and work through unresolved issues. It's a mirror reflecting our internal world, providing insight into how we relate to others and ourselves.

Ultimately, psychoanalytic theory presents the self as a deep well of thoughts, impulses, and memories, all interwoven to create the tapestry of our psyche. It's a view that emphasizes the complexity of human nature, the internal struggles that define us, and the potential for self-awareness and transformation.

Yet, psychoanalysis is not without its critics. Some argue it places too much emphasis on the unconscious, on childhood, on the darker aspects of our psyche. But whether one sees it as a key to understanding the self or a flawed map of the human mind, its influence on psychology—and our quest to understand ourselves—can't be denied.

In our fast-paced world, where the external often takes precedence, psychoanalytic perspectives invite us to slow down, to turn inward. They remind us that understanding the self is not a quick journey; it's an ongoing exploration. One that requires patience, courage, and an openness to the unknown.

So we continue to delve into our inner selves, guided by the insights of psychoanalysis. We navigate the waters of our unconscious, confronting dragons and discovering treasures within. It's often a solitary voyage, but it's one that can lead to the most profound discoveries.

The inner self is a landscape rich with meaning, a complex puzzle waiting to be understood. Psychoanalytic theory provides us with a lantern to illuminate the path. It's up to us to walk it, to explore the depths of our psyche with curiosity and resolve. For in understanding the inner self, we unlock the potential for growth, healing, and a deeper connection to the world around us.

In the grand tapestry of psychological perspectives, the psychoanalytic view holds a unique thread. It weaves the notion that within us lies an intricate, often conflicted, inner world. A world worth exploring, worth understanding, for in its depths lies the key to our truest self.

Chapter 5:
The Social Self

We're social creatures, it's how we're wired; the fabric of society itself weaves into the individual essence, molding identities with invisible threads. Within this chapter, we unpack the intricate dance between self and society, exploring how cultural tapestries and the subtle nuances of interaction embroider the core of our being. It's a narrative as old as time—our roles, language, the collective gaze—all shaping the tapestry of the "I" within a sprawling "we". Yet, within this interplay, a question surfaces like a breath: How much of me is truly mine? This narrative isn't linear, but a mosaic made from fragments of every person we've met, every word we've absorbed. Peer influence, that invisible force, nudges our trajectory in unseen ways, and group identity—this concept we nestle into for comfort or, sometimes, hide within for fear of standing apart. But here lies the crux; it's a mirror reflecting how seamlessly society's expectations can sculpt the bedrock of our individuality, often cloaking the authentic self.

Nevertheless, this chapter isn't a tale of capitulation to social constructs but a call to awareness. Understanding is the first step, they say. To recognize the external forces at play is to begin the journey of reclaiming the self that whispers beneath the roles we perform. This is the essence of the social self—not a singular entity but a multitude of voices, some ours, some borrowed, all harmonizing into the symphony that is "me".

The Impact of Society and Culture

It shapes us, molds us like clay. The tendrils of society and culture weave through the essence of our being, whispering who we ought to be, what to desire, where we belong. We're born into a world rich with history, norms, and expectations, yet we seldom pause to question their origin or their hold on us. The food we eat, the clothes we wear, words that roll off our tongue - all stitched into the fabric of our identity by invisible hands. Yet, within this tapestry lies a paradox; it's both a prison and a playground. Society's mirror reflects myriad possibilities, each glance offering a different shade of ourselves, influenced by the zeitgeist, the collective psyche pulsing through the ages. As working professionals, navigating the dichotomy between individuality and conformity becomes our daily dance. We adjust our masks, juggling roles, sometimes losing sight of where the role ends and the self begins. Amidst this interplay of forces, the question arises - can we truly know ourselves outside the societal gaze? Perhaps in understanding the sway of culture, we begin the journey of unwinding, peeling back layers to reveal the core, unadulterated self, waiting like a silent observer. It's a solitary path, lined with the echoes of all who walked before, whispering the age-old reminder that the only constant in life is change, and in change, there lies the opportunity for discovery.

Socialization Processes

We wander through life, absorbing bits and pieces of the world around us. It shapes us, molds us into beings with thoughts and feelings influenced by an unseen force. This force, often unnoticed, steers the course of our lives from the shadows. It's called socialization.

Think of socialization as the air we breathe. It's everywhere, yet it goes unnoticed until it changes or disappears. From the moment we're born, the process begins. It teaches us the norms, values, beliefs, and behaviors of our society. Like a river carving its path through rock, socialization shapes our identities, guides our thoughts, and influences our decisions.

Socialization isn't a simple one-way street. It's a complex highway with multiple lanes and directions. There's the family, often our first teachers, showing us love, discipline, and the basics of human interaction. Then there's the school, where we're exposed to new ideas, different cultures, and the essence of cooperation and competition. And let's not forget the broader society with its media, traditions, and laws, painting the larger picture of the world.

Each of these elements plays a crucial role. They intermingle, sometimes clashing, sometimes harmonizing, to produce the unique melody that is the self. But this process, it's not static. It evolves. As society changes, so does the way we are socialized. Technology, for instance, has introduced new realms of socialization, changing how we perceive the world and ourselves.

The workplace, a haven for adults, serves as yet another classroom for socialization. It's where we learn the unwritten rules of power, negotiation, and professional identity. The roles we assume, whether chosen or bestowed upon us, dictate vast portions of our daily interactions and self-perception.

Peer groups too, they wield power. They offer a sense of belonging, a mirror reflecting our own selves in the context of the larger world. They shape our tastes, our habits, even the way we speak. Their influence can be subtle, a gentle nudging towards conformity, or a powerful tide, pulling us into the depths of group identity.

And then there are the moments of resistance, where the self pushes back against the forces of socialization. These moments, often overlooked, are vital. They're the instances where personal values clash with societal expectations, where the self asserts its uniqueness.

Socialization is perpetual, a lifelong journey. It adjusts with age, experience, and changing societal landscapes. What was once an agent of socialization can evolve, or fade into the background, replaced by new structures, new media, new norms.

Consider love. It's more than a feeling; it's a lesson in socialization. Through love, we learn empathy, sacrifice, the joy of giving. It's a force that transcends cultural borders, teaching us lessons universal in their appeal yet personal in their application.

However, socialization can also construct barriers. Gender, race, class, and ethnicity can limit or define the ways we're allowed to interact with the world. These categories, though social constructs, have real-world implications, shaping our experiences and opportunities.

Thus, understanding the socialization process is crucial. It illuminates the path to understanding ourselves and the society we inhabit. It unlocks the door to empathy, allowing us to appreciate the complexities of human identity. It guides us in questioning norms, challenging unjust structures, and embracing diversity.

The task then falls to us. To be mindful of how we're being shaped, to seek out diverse experiences, to question and understand the forces that mold us. It's a journey of constant learning, of deconstructing and reconstructing the self, in an effort to live authentically in a world that ceaselessly tries to define us.

We are, after all, social creatures. We crave connection, understanding, a place in the broader tapestry of human society. And so, we must navigate the socialization process with both caution and curiosity, recognizing its power to shape the self, and seizing opportunities to mold it in our own image.

In the end, socialization is about connection. It's the thread that ties the individual to the collective, the self to the society. It's a dance, sometimes graceful, sometimes awkward, but always moving. And as we dance, we learn. About the world, about each other, about ourselves.

So let's take a step back, observe the dance from the sidelines, then step back in with renewed purpose. Let's embrace the processes that shape us, while striving to shape them in return. Because in understanding socialization, we understand a fundamental part of the human condition, and in doing so, we unlock the full potential of the self.

The Role of Language

We tread along this exploration of self, stepping past the thresholds of consciousness, society, and psychology. Now, we veer towards the architecture of language. It's not merely a tool for communication, but a cornerstone in the construction of the self. Language shapes thought, molds consciousness, and forges identities. It's the scaffold on which societies are built and through which cultures breathe.

Consider a newborn, pure and unmarked by the world's script. As language is introduced, it begins to shape perception. Words classify the abstract and the concrete, drawing boundaries where none existed. A child doesn't see blue because they're born knowing 'blue'. They learn it, encapsulate a spectrum of wavelengths into a word, and suddenly the world is a rainbow. Language is not just descriptive. It is prescriptive, casting reality in its terms.

Language is the lens through which we view others and ourselves. It mirrors the prevailing culture, embodying its values, biases, and norms. Through language, social hierarchies are maintained, and power dynamics are communicated. It's no coincidence that Orwell's dystopia hinged on 'Newspeak'. Control the language, and you control thought; control thought, and you control the self.

Yet, language is fluid, a testament to the ever-changing self. It evolves, discards the obsolete, and embraces the new. Slang, jargon, and even professional lingo, are not just linguistic novelties. They're indicators of shifting identities, of groups forming and reforming around new axes of understanding. Language, then, is not static. It is dynamic, much like the self.

In conversations, the currency of words is spent not just to exchange information but to negotiate identities. The 'I' that speaks is not constant but tailored. It shifts, adapts, and responds to the 'You' that listens. Language in this dialogue is both a bridge and a barrier. It is through speech that we express our innermost thoughts, yet it is also through language that we conceal, manipulate, and obfuscate.

The medium of language extends beyond the spoken into the written. Here, the self finds a canvas as broad as thought itself. Writing allows for reflection, a conversation with an unseen, perhaps future, other. It is in this dialogue that many find their truest voice. The pen, in crafting narratives, crafts the self.

Cultural narratives, those grand stories a society tells itself, are imbued with language's power. Myths, legends, and histories shape collective identities, telling us who we are, where we come from, and what we value. They are the lexicon of culture, and as members of that culture, we find our place within that narrative. The self, in this sense, is both author and character in the societal story.

Language, however, has its limitations. It can box us in, trap us in categories and labels. The words we have at our disposal can both define and confine. In recognizing this, there's liberation. The search for new words, new languages even, is a testament to the human spirit's refusal to be caged. It is through this search that the self expands, reaching into the ineffable.

Language also divides. It can be a source of unity, yes, but also of misunderstanding and conflict. The nuances of meaning, the subtleties of tone, can all too easily be lost, especially in a globalized world where cultures collide. Yet, in this chaos, there lies opportunity. For it is through the struggle to understand and to be understood that we often find our deepest connections with others.

Consider how language shapes memory. The stories we tell ourselves about ourselves are all couched in language. These narratives solidify into the identity we carry. Alter the language, change the story, and the self is remade. Memory, then, is not a static vault but a dynamic play, one where language is both playwright and actor.

But what of silence? Silence, too, speaks. It's powerful precisely because it stands outside of language, yet it shapes the spaces between words, giving them weight and meaning. Silence can be a form of resistance, a refusal to partake in the prevailing discourse. It can also be introspective, a pause in the constant stream of thought and speech, allowing for a different kind of self-awareness.

Language and thought are entwined, yes, but language also shapes emotion. The words we have for our feelings influence how we experience them. Consider the richness of language's vocabulary for sorrow across cultures. Each word provides a nuance, a shade of meaning that deepens the tapestry of human experience. Emotion, like self, is linguistically constructed.

Now, consider the role of language in technology. The digital age has spawned new languages, from programming codes that shape our digital worlds to the shorthand of texts and tweets that shape our social interactions. These languages, too, mold the self, creating new identities, communities, and ways of relating to one another and to the world.

In exploring the role of language, we uncover the complexity of the self. Language is not merely a tool for expressing thought but a force that shapes thought, identity, and reality itself. To understand the self, we must grapple with language, its powers, and its limitations. In the architecture of language, we find the blueprint of the self.

The journey of self-discovery is, in many ways, a linguistic journey. It's about finding the words to express who we are, who we've been, and who we wish to become. This quest for expression, for comprehension, is at the heart of what it means to be human. As we delve deeper into the realms of language, we find not just the contours of our individual selves but the communal tapestry that binds us all.

Peer Influence and Group Identity

There's something about the way we sway in the direction where the majority of heads are turning. It's like a dance we're all part of, sometimes knowingly, often blindly. Peer influence, it's a force more potent than we give it credit for. It shapes, molds, pushes, and pulls. We find ourselves amidst these invisible tides that guide our sense of self, our identity within the groups we orbit.

The person you are at work, isn't that a version tempered by the expectations and norms of your professional peers? There's a script we follow, unwritten but understood. We dress a certain way, speak in certain terms, and align our values, often subconsciously, with those around us. This isn't about losing authenticity but about finding our place in the social fabric that surrounds us.

Think of the last time you were with friends, laughter spilling like wine, conversations meandering through the vineyards of past memories and future dreams. Did you notice how your gestures, your language, even your opinions aligned with the group's ethos? This mirroring isn't mimicry but a form of social survival, an instinctual blend into the collective identity.

Group identity does more than dictate the superficial aspects of our lives. It goes deeper, carving out the channels through which our beliefs and values flow. It's both a refuge and a prison. Safe within the walls of common understanding, we sometimes hesitate to peek over, fearful of what lies beyond the comfort of conformity.

But here's where the plot thickens. Within each group, there are subcurrents, undercurrents, hidden eddies of individuality. Standing on the shoreline of our consciousness is the desire for individual expression. It's this tension between the urge to belong and the need to be unique that crafts the elaborate tapestry of the self.

It's crucial, then, to navigate these waters with awareness. Recognizing the influence of peers and groups isn't about rejecting it wholesale. It's about discerning which parts of our group identity serve us and which parts stifle our individuality.

Peer influence can uplift, inspire, and motivate. It can drive us to heights we might not reach on our own. The encouragement of a colleague, the support of friends—these are the winds beneath the wings of our aspirations. But like all winds, they can shift, sometimes blowing us off course. The art lies in adjusting our sails, in learning when to go with the flow and when to cut across the current.

Group identity can be a beacon, illuminating common ground and fostering a sense of belonging. Yet, what happens when that beacon becomes a fence? When the fear of being cast out overrides the truth of who we are? It's a delicate balance, finding unity without losing oneself in the process.

Adaptation is a survival skill, honed through eons of evolution. We adapt to the norms and expectations of our groups, often without conscious thought. But every adaptation is a choice, whether we acknowledge it or not. The challenge is to make these choices consciously, shaping our social selves with intention rather than inertia.

Consider the moments when you've stood at the crossroads of conformity and authenticity. The pressure to conform is a gravitational pull, rooted in our primal fear of exclusion. Yet, there's a quiet power in authenticity, in the courage to express the nuances of our individuality within the tapestry of group identity.

Self-awareness is the compass that guides us through these social seas. It's what allows us to recognize the difference between adapting and assimilating, between belonging and losing ourselves. With self-awareness, we can appreciate the influence of peers and groups while anchoring our sense of self in the bedrock of our values and beliefs.

The dance of the social self is intricate, a step forward into group identity, a step back into individuality. It's a dance we all partake in, consciously or not. The key, perhaps, is to dance with intention, with an awareness of the music and the steps, with a mindful presence that honors both the group and the self.

In the end, peer influence and group identity are not forces to be resisted or resented. They're elements of the human experience to be navigated with wisdom and compassion. They shape us, but they don't define us. Our journey is one of constant negotiation, of finding the balance that allows us to belong without becoming lost.

So, as we move through the landscapes of our social selves, let's do so with eyes wide open. Let's recognize the power of peer influence and the resonance of group identity, but let's also honor the call of our unique voice within the chorus. It's in this balance that we find the truest expression of ourselves, individually and together.

Perhaps, then, the question isn't how we can escape the influence of peers or shed our group identities. Maybe the real question is how we can navigate these waters with grace, integrating the external with the internal, in a way that enriches both our collective existence and our personal essence. It's a journey worth taking, a dance worth learning.

Chapter 6:
The Emotional Self

In exploring the tapestry that is the self, we come to the threads of emotion, vibrant and volatile, painting our inner world with hues of joy, sadness, fear, and anger. Emotions, not just mere reactions but a core component of our identity, weave through our existence, influencing not just how we view the world, but how we place ourselves within it. This chapter delves into the intricate relationship between emotion and self-identity, an interplay that shapes our perceptions, decisions, and interactions. The spectrum of emotions extends far beyond the basic, touching every facet of our lives, yet it's our emotional intelligence – our capacity to recognize, understand, and manage these emotions – that truly defines the emotional self. It's here, in the grasp of our feelings, we uncover the depth of our sensibility, the starkness of our humanity. Do we navigate our emotional seas with the deft touch of a seasoned captain, or are we adrift, at the mercy of every storm? It's a quest not for the faint of heart, but for those daring to venture into the realm of self-discovery, it's a journey worth embarking on. As we peel back the layers, we find that our emotions, once thought to be wild and untamed, can be understood, guiding us to a richer, more nuanced understanding of who we are.

Emotions as a Component of the Self

Emotions weave through our lives, coloring perceptions, dictating actions. They're not just reactions; they're a fundamental part of who we are. Think about it. Joy, fear, love, anger. They shape decisions, change directions. They're the undercurrent of every thought, the backdrop of every moment. Sometimes subtle, sometimes overwhelming. But always there. Part of the self, as much as the mind or body. It's not just about feeling. It's deeper. Emotions connect us to others, to the world. They remind us we're alive. Look closer. It's not just happiness or sorrow. It's the nuance, the complexity. Anger can spur change. Sadness can deepen empathy. We're a mosaic of these emotions, a composition unique to each. Yet, they unite us too. Shared joy, shared grief. In understanding our emotions, we glimpse the core of self, the essence that makes us human. It's a journey inward, exploring not just what we think, but what we feel. It's about acknowledging these emotions, recognizing their power, their role in the tapestry of self.

The Spectrum of Emotions

We've traversed the landscapes of the self, mapping out territories from neurons to notions, from the cradle of consciousness to social constructs. Now, we edge closer to the heart's core, to the spectrum of emotions that paint our days with the hues of humanity.

Emotions, elusive and yet so integral. They're the whispers and roars within, shaping perceptions, driving actions. We feel before we think, they say. And it's true. Emotions are our first responders, alert to the world's stimuli, quick to prepare us for what's next. They are the primal music to which our rational thoughts choreograph their dance.

Their range is vast. Joy, sorrow, fear, love—each a note on the emotional keyboard, available to be played in endless combinations. The spectrum is fluid, moving us from one state to another, often without notice. One moment, joy bubbles like champagne, the next, sorrow drowns us like a tide. It's a spectrum because there's no clear separation, no hard lines. Only a gradual blending, a flowing from one emotion into another.

Consider anger. It's often misjudged, labeled as purely negative. Yet, at its core, anger is a cry for change, a passionate assertion that something is amiss. It can be the fire that fuels action, the force that pushes us to solve problems, to stand up for what's right.

Then there's fear, the great conservator. It can paralyze, yes, but it also protects. It's the primal signal to tread carefully, to avoid harm. Fear is not an enemy; it's a survival mechanism, honed by evolution, guardian of the physical self.

Love, in contrast, is the ultimate unifier. It dissolves boundaries, fosters empathy, nourishes the spirit. It can be as tranquil as a quiet sunrise or as tumultuous as a stormy sea. It's a force that propels us, sometimes into joy, sometimes into sorrow.

Joy itself is that fleeting peak, the summit of the emotional landscape. It's pure and uplifting, a light that brightens everything around. And yet, its very transience teaches us appreciation, the need to embrace moments before they slip away.

Sorrow, the deep valley, has its place too. It carves into us spaces for empathy, for understanding. It makes us human in the most profound way, teaching resilience, endurance, the capacity to find light in the darkest tunnels.

Between these peaks and valleys lie myriad nuances. Hope, anticipation, nostalgia, envy—each adding depth and complexity to the human experience. The spectrum is wide, intricate, a testament to our capacity for feeling, for being.

But why this spectrum? Why not a simpler, more navigable emotional landscape? Because emotions are the language of the self, a means to communicate with ourselves and with the world. They are indicators, messengers. They tell us when to pause, when to push forward, when to protect ourselves, and when to connect with others.

Understanding this spectrum requires mindfulness. It's about tuning in, listening to the emotions as they rise and fall, without immediate judgment. It's about acknowledging their presence, their validity, even when they're uncomfortable.

Emotional intelligence, then, is the skill of navigating this spectrum. It's recognizing what we feel, understanding why we feel it, and deciding how we respond. It's the art of managing our emotions, of using their energy constructively, without being overrun by their force.

Every emotion has its place, its utility, its beauty. The spectrum of emotions is a canvas, and we, with our lives, are the artists. We blend, we contrast, we create our masterpieces amid joy and sorrow, love and fear.

And so, we come to see that emotional self-mastery is not about suppression or avoidance but about balance and understanding. It's embracing the full spectrum, from the darkest shades to the brightest tones. It's recognizing that within this spectrum lies the essence of our humanity, the depth of our self.

This journey through the spectrum of emotions isn't just about introspection. It's a path to a richer, more empathetic engagement with the world. As we understand our own emotions, we deepen our ability to connect with others, to see beneath the surface, to communicate with compassion and clarity.

In the grand tapestry of the self, emotions are vibrant threads, weaving together experiences, memories, choices. They color our perceptions, influence our decisions, bind us to others. They are the music of our internal worlds, the rhythm of our lives. And as we learn to listen, to understand, to conduct this music with grace, we find our way closer to the essence of who we are.

Emotional Intelligence

It cuts deep. More than intellect. More than skills honed over decades. It's how you interpret the world.

How the world interprets you. Ripples caused by emotional currents, both under and on the surface.

In the sprawl of consciousness, we recognize the self. But the emotional self? It's a nebula within the neural cosmos. Here, emotional intelligence shines as a pivotal beacon. It's not about taming emotions, but understanding them. Recognizing their origins. Their impacts. On ourselves. On others.

Emotional intelligence is the bridge. Between thought and feeling. Between impulse and understanding. It's the ability to navigate the turbulent waters of our internal seas and to forecast the weather in others'. To understand and manage our emotions, and to perceive and influence the emotions of those around us.

Imagine the brain. The limbic system, to be specific. It's where emotions brew. But what do we do with this brew? Does it intoxicate us or nourish us? Emotional intelligence is the sobriety test. It's not just in our heads. It's in our actions. Our connections. Our failures and our triumphs.

Within the chaos of neurons firing, where does emotional intelligence fit? It's the order in the chaos. The ability to pause. Reflect. Choose. It's a muscle, flexed not in isolation but in every interaction, every thought, every breath.

And what of its roots? Like trees, emotions have roots deep and tangled. Emotional intelligence is the process of gently excavating these roots. Understanding not just the 'what' but the 'why'. It transforms the soil of our being, making it fertile for growth.

In the relentless march of days, among storms and calm, emotional intelligence is our compass. It directs us not just towards external success, but towards internal equilibrium. It's a journey inward as much as outward. From self-awareness to self-regulation. From empathy to social skills.

We're social beings. Threads in a larger tapestry. Emotional intelligence is the skill of weaving these threads without fraying. It's recognizing the texture of each thread, its strength, its weaknesses. And in this recognition, there is understanding. Compassion. Connection.

In the workplace, its value is unmatched. The leader who understands not just the task, but the team. The colleague who listens, not just hears. In a world where our worth is often quantified by the tangibles, emotional intelligence reminds us of the power of the intangibles.

It's a mistake to consider emotions as secondary. As distractions. They are the essence of our humanity.

They drive us. Shape us. Emotional intelligence is not the suppression of this truth but the embracing of it. It's living fully, with awareness and intent.

Emotional intelligence is a dance. A dance of balance between heart and mind. It's not about controlling emotions but about understanding their language. It's about listening to the quietest whispers of our hearts with the full attention of our minds.

The journey of emotional intelligence begins with a single, yet profound step: self-awareness. It's looking into the mirror of our soul, not with judgment, but with curiosity. It's recognizing our emotional triggers and the stories we tell ourselves about what they mean.

Self-regulation follows. It's about choosing our response instead of being captive to our reactions. It's the pause between stimulus and response. A moment of choice where emotional intelligence thrives.

Empathy is our bridge to others. It's feeling with, not just for. It's understanding the emotional landscapes of others from their perspective. It's a fundamental human connection, facilitated by emotional intelligence.

And finally, emotional intelligence is about social skills. It's navigating the complexities of human relationships with grace and understanding. It's fostering environments where emotional honesty and authenticity can flourish. It's about building bridges, not walls, with our fellow humans.

So, as we journey through the chapters of understanding the self, remember this: emotional intelligence is not just a segment of this exploration. It is the thread weaving through each aspect of our being, reinforcing the tapestry of our existence with resilience, empathy, and a profound understanding of the depth of our emotional selves.

Chapter 7:
Identity and Role Playing

The masks are many, the stage vast, and we, the actors, juggle identities with the ease of a practiced hand. Yet, what compels us to slip in and out of these roles with such fluidity? Is it necessity, or perhaps the unvoiced expectation of those around us? In the realm of our professional lives, the cloak of competency and efficiency is often donned, a necessary guise to navigate the competitive waters of industry. Yet, this mask seldom remains outside the confines of the office; it morphs as we step into the warmth of personal relationships. Here, a different facet of the self comes to the forefront, softer, perhaps more genuine, but a role, nonetheless. The dance between authenticity and societal expectation continues, an intricate ballet of self and identity. But where does the essence of the self reside in this maze of roles? Is it at the core, a steadfast anchor, or does it too, shift and sway with the winds of circumstance? The quest for authenticity, a beacon in the night, guides us, yet the path is wrought with the shadows of expectation. The question then becomes, not who we are, but who we choose to be amidst the myriad roles we play.

The Many Faces We Wear

Every day, we step into the world cloaked in roles as if they're our second skin. These roles, vast and varied, shape our interactions, molding the self that we present to the outside. At work, we don the mantle of professionalism, our actions and words tempered by the expectations of our role. With friends and family, another mask slips on, one that's perhaps more casual, freer but still constrained by unspoken social contracts. It's a dance, intricate and complex, where each step, each turn, embodies a different aspect of who we are— or at least, who we wish to be seen as. Yet, amidst this constant shifting, a question surfaces, subtle but persistent. Who are we beneath these layers? Are these faces just parts to be played, or do they, in their repetition, become facets of a deeper truth about ourselves? This oscillation between authenticity and performance, it's more than mere role-playing; it's a fundamental aspect of the human condition, compelling us to navigate the murky waters between our true selves and the selves we perform. It's a journey fraught with discovery and disillusionment, each face we wear a testament to our search for identity in a world that relentlessly asks us who we are.

Professional Identity

It brews in the essence of what we do, shapes in the tasks we undertake, and solidifies with each decision we make. It's like a shadow, subtle yet distinctly ours. Who are we in the realms of our profession? What mirrors back when we gaze into the waters of our career?

In the early mornings, before the world stirs to life, a question lingers in the air. It's faint, almost a whisper. "Who am I in my profession?" This question, it's not just about what we do. It's deeper. It's about the fabric of our being woven into our work.

The concept of professional identity isn't linear. It's not a path trodden by many. It's unique, like footprints on a beach, washed away and made anew with every tide. Our roles, tasks, and titles, they shape this identity, yet it's more than the sum of these parts.

Consider the roles we inhabit. Each one, a brick in the edifice of our professional selves. With each role, we adapt, we change. We're actors on a stage, but the script is unwritten, crafted by our experiences, skills, and interactions.

And then, there's the crucible of challenge. Adversity acts as a forge for our professional identity. Each setback, every failure, is not just a stumbling block. It's an opportunity to reshape, to reforge ourselves in the fires of our trials.

But what of our successes? They, too, shape us. Each achievement, a thread woven into the tapestry of our professional identity. They bolster confidence, contour our self-perception, and direct our journey onwards.

Peers and mentors cast long shadows on our path. Their influence, subtle yet profound, molds our professional identity. They are mirrors reflecting our potential, windows into what we could become.

Over time, our professional identity evolves. It's not static, not a photograph but a painting, ever-changing with each stroke of our careers. The roles we once held, the challenges we've faced, the successes we've savored, all contribute to this relentless transformation.

Yet, there's a constant quest for authenticity within this evolution. How do we remain true to ourselves in a world that often demands we wear masks? It's a delicate dance, a balancing act between societal expectations and the authentic self.

In this pursuit, integrity becomes our north star. It guides us through the fog of conformity, illuminating a path that aligns our professional actions with our inner values. Integrity ensures that our professional identity doesn't stray too far from who we truly are.

Change, inevitable and constant, tests our professional identity. New technologies, evolving societal norms, and personal growth all demand adaptation. Yet, within this flux, our core remains, a lighthouse amidst the changing tides of our professional landscape.

Reflection, then, serves as our compass. Amidst the bustle of deadlines and meetings, pausing to reflect is akin to breathing. It's in these moments of quiet introspection that we truly see the contours of our professional identity, shaped by our actions, refined by our choices.

As the days blend into years, and the years into a career, a narrative emerges. This story, our professional journey, is a mosaic of successes and failures, challenges and triumphs. Each piece, a testament to our growth, our resilience, and our ever-evolving professional identity.

So, who are we in the realms of our profession? We're seekers and learners, shaped by our experiences, guided by our values, and driven by a quest for meaning. Our professional identity, complex and multifaceted, is a reflection of this journey. A journey not just of what we do, but who we become in the process.

In the quiet of the night, as we ponder our place in the professional world, the answer comes in whispers, in reflections, in the quiet understanding that our professional identity is not just about the work we do. It's about the person we choose to be, day in, day out, in pursuit of our passions, in alignment with our values, and in service to something greater than ourselves.

Personal Relationships and Self

Relationships shape us. We start as mirrors, reflecting those closest. In tender ages, our first bonds sculpt the clay of our being. Later, peers press their own shapes into ours. But what of the self amidst these forms?

Consider love. In love, two selves converge. Or so the story goes. Yet often, love demands a self-sacrifice, a tempering of one's essence to mold with another. The question then, is this merging a loss of self or an expansion? Love tests the boundaries of our individuality, blurring lines we thought clear. But therein lies love's gift – the discovery of depths within us, unknown chambers of our heart and spirit that only another's touch can reveal.

Friendship, too, is a mirror, but of another kind. It reflects not what we lack but what we are. True friends see our light and dark and love both. They remind us of who we are when we forget. This reflection strengthens our self, solidifies our identity amidst change. Friendship offers a ground on which to stand firm yet encourages our wings to unfold.

Family ties, however, weave a complex tapestry. Here is where our first self is molded, our first understanding of love and identity born. Amidst the familial weave, we often find our most unyieldable selves, but also the selves we wish to outgrow. Tension between familial expectations and personal truth can chafe. Yet, it's this friction that can polish our truest self, emerging only after struggle.

Work, unexpectedly, becomes a crucible for self-discovery. Professional relationships demand masks, roles to play. Yet, each role, each mask worn or discarded, teaches us. We learn the fluidity of self, how it can adapt. Yet, beneath these roles, the core self watches, learns, and sometimes, waits to re-emerge.

Conflict, inevitably, is the anvil on which personal relationships and the self are forged. In conflict, our deepest selves shout, whisper, and quiver. Here we discover our resilience, our capacity for forgiveness and understanding, or our harbored resentments. Each conflict navigated reshapes us, sometimes subtly, sometimes profoundly. It reveals our strengths and uncovers our vulnerabilities, urging growth.

Isolation, too, has its teachings. In the absence of others, we meet our naked self, stripped of roles, expectations, and reflections. Solitude offers a mirror of a different kind, one that reflects not others' perceptions but our own. Here lies the terrain for profound self-discovery, for in silence, the voice of our true self speaks loudest.

Change, constant and inevitable, tests the self in the arena of relationships. As we evolve, so do our connections. Some grow with us, stretching into new forms. Others, once close, drift into memory. Each shift offers a choice – to cling to the past or to embrace the present person we've become. Through change, relationships become both map and compass, guiding our continuous journey of self-discovery.

Trust, fragile and essential, binds the self to another. It's in trust that we allow ourselves to be vulnerable, to show our hidden selves. With trust comes the freedom to be authentic, to lower the masks. It's through vulnerability that we invite deeper connection, fostering stronger bonds that nourish our true selves.

Communication, the bridge between selves, holds the power to build or break. It's through sharing our thoughts, our feelings, our fears, and our dreams that we reveal our inner world. Effective communication deepens understanding, not just of the other, but of ourselves. In articulating our innermost selves, we learn, we grow, and sometimes, we surprise ourselves.

Authenticity, the pursuit of many but the achievement of few, is the crown of personal relationships. To be authentic is to be raw, to expose the unpolished self to another's gaze. It's a risky venture, for in revealing our true selves, we risk rejection. But the reward is a connection untainted by pretense, a bond that can endure the tests of time and change.

Compassion, extended to others and to oneself, softens the journey. In understanding the flaws and struggles of another, we learn to forgive our own. Compassion bridges the gap between differing selves, allowing empathy to flourish. In this space, relationships thrive, forged in the understanding that all of us are works in progress, seeking, learning, growing.

Balance, elusive and essential, is the quest in the dance of personal relationships and the self. To give without losing oneself, to receive without becoming dependent. It's a delicate act, this balance, requiring constant adjustment, a keen awareness of self and other. Yet, it is within this balance that our deepest connections are found, connections that honor both our shared humanity and our individual uniqueness.

In reflecting on personal relationships and the self, we see a landscape rich and varied, fraught with challenge but also brimming with potential. These connections, in their many forms, guide us, shape us, and ultimately, reveal us. For in the end, it is through our relationships that we discover the vastness of our selves, a universe within, ever expanding, infinite in its depths.

Authenticity vs. Social Expectations

The line between who we are and who we're expected to be is often blurred. It's a dance between the authentic self and the version of us that society demands. Each step, each movement, is measured, sometimes calculated, often instinctive. We wear masks. Sometimes they're so comfortable we forget we have them on. Other times, they chafe, reminding us of the dichotomy between our inner world and the external one.

In the realm of work, this juxtaposition becomes pronounced. A professional identity evolves—an amalgam of societal expectations, job requirements, and personal ambitions. It's a suit tailored to fit the occasion, yet sometimes it feels like it belongs to someone else. We're applauded for playing our roles well, for fulfilling tasks with proficiency. Yet, in silent moments, we ponder if the role consumes the self.

Personal relationships, too, are arenas for this intricate dance. With family, with friends, with partners. Each relationship calls forth a different facet of our being. The question of authenticity here becomes a balancing act. How much of ourselves do we reveal? How much do we withhold for peace, for love, for harmony? It's a give and take—an act of negotiation between our true selves and the selves we present to maintain connections.

Social expectations are like shifting sands— constantly changing, evolving with the times. What was once deemed essential can suddenly become obsolete. The pressure to keep up, to mold ourselves into ever new shapes can be exhausting. It begs the question, where does one draw the line? At what point does the alteration of self for social acceptance stop, and the assertion of authenticity begin?

Authenticity—it's a concept as revered as it is feared. To be authentic is to strip away the pretenses, to stand in our truth. It's an act of bravery in a world that often rewards conformity. Yet, it's also a source of power. To navigate life from a place of authenticity is to wield a form of freedom that no societal expectation can quench.

But the pursuit of authenticity isn't bereft of its trials. It can lead to isolation, to misunderstandings. Being true to oneself in the face of societal norms that dictate otherwise is a path fraught with challenges. Yet, those who choose to walk it find a sense of self that is unshakeable, unwavering.

The dialogue between authenticity and social expectations is ongoing. It's a conversation that each of us must engage in. The nuances, the subtleties—it's all part of the human experience. To know when to conform and when to stand firm in our authenticity is a skill. It's an art.

One might wonder, then, how does one cultivate this art? It begins with self-awareness. To know oneself deeply is the first step toward navigating the complexities of this dual existence. It's about being mindful of the masks we wear and having the courage to take them off when they no longer serve us.

It's also about compassion—compassion for oneself and for others. We're all engaged in this dance, after all. Each person we meet is grappling with their own dichotomies. To extend understanding, to offer space for authenticity in others as we seek it for ourselves, is to build bridges where walls once might have stood.

Embracing vulnerability is another key. Authenticity cannot coexist with invulnerability. To be authentic is to be open about our flaws, our mistakes, our fears. It's about allowing ourselves to be seen, truly seen, by those around us. This vulnerability, though scary, is the very thing that connects us, that makes us human.

Yet, it's important to recognize that authenticity is not an excuse for unkindness or thoughtlessness. It's not about airing every grievance or sharing every thought unfiltered. True authenticity is considerate; it respects boundaries—our own and those of others.

As we journey through life, the interplay between authenticity and social expectations remains a constant companion. It's a theme that recurs, in different guises, at different stages of our journey. Each encounter with it is an opportunity for growth, for deeper understanding, for greater alignment with our true selves.

Ultimately, the choice between authenticity and social conformity is a personal one. It's a decision that each of us must make, again and again, as we navigate the complexities of life. But one thing remains clear: in the pursuit of authenticity, in the quest to align more closely with our true selves, there lies the path to genuine fulfillment and peace.

So, we move forward, masks in hand, aware of the play but not consumed by it. We learn, we grow, we evolve—striving always for that delicate balance between being true to ourselves and meeting the expectations of the world around us. It's not an easy journey, but it's one worth taking. For in the dance between authenticity and social expectations, we find not just ourselves, but also our place in the wider tapestry of human connection.

Chapter 8:
Memory and the Self

In the story of who we are, memory stitches patches of experiences into a coherent narrative. Each fragment, a recall, a moment lived, shapes the contours of our identity. Yet, the act of remembering is less a replay, more a re-creation; our minds, artists painting over old lines with each recall. The self, then, is an art piece constantly in progress, a collage of memories curated by the mind's eye. Memories are not static; they morph, fade, and sometimes disappear, leaving spaces we fill with new interpretations, new narratives. This fluidity blurs the lines between what was and what is remembered as was, challenging our perceptions of the immutable self. In the churning waters of memory, we find that forgetting is not a loss but a transformation, an essential process in the remaking of the self. We navigate through life, collecting, discarding, and reshaping memories, sculpting ourselves anew with each dawn. And in this perpetual motion, we glimpse the essence of identity not as a monolith but as a river - ever flowing, ever changing, yet always unmistakably our own.

The Role of Memory in Identity

Memory stitches the tapestry of our self. It's the thread that connects who we were, who we are, and who we'll become. We grasp at memories, fleeting and fragile, piecing together the narrative of our identity. Each memory, a brush stroke on the vast canvas of our psyche. Without them, identity diffuses into the ether, unanchored and formless. Memory shapes our reactions, our loves, our fears. It's a garden where past mistakes and triumphs grow side by side, each leaf a lesson, every flower a chapter of our story. The mind, a curator, selects and discards, molding identity with the subtlety of a sculptor. We are, in essence, collections of memories, compilations of moments that, together, whisper who we are. But memories are not static; they shift, evolve, and fade, rendering our sense of self a perpetual work in progress. The role of memory in identity is not just about preservation but transformation, a dynamic interplay that crafts the evolving saga of the self.

Personal Narratives

We each tell ourselves stories. They shape the contours of our lives. They're crafted in the mind's eye, marred by the grit of experience. From birth to the brink of now, a narrative emerges. We're the sum of these narratives, aren't we? Each one a brush stroke on the canvas of the self.

Think about the first story you remember telling yourself. A narrative so simple yet so defining. Was it the story of victory, perhaps in the schoolyard? Or was it one of loss, the first pet or grandparent, slipping away into memories? Such narratives lay the foundation.

Life moves. We collect these stories. A tapestry emerges with hues both dark and bright. It's in the way we carry our past, in the invisible knapsack of experience, where our personal narratives reside. These echoes shape how we view the world, how we view ourselves.

Work shapes us differently. It molds narratives of success, of failure, of enduring monotony. Think of the first job. The smell of the place. The feel of the task. The faces. All of it, a new chapter. It spoke to us, whispered of what we could become, what we refused to be.

Relationships intertwine with our self-narratives, complexifying them. Love found. Love lost. Friendship that withstood the test of time. Or bonds that frayed under tension. Each encounter, a line in our ongoing self-story, adding depth, sometimes pain, enriching the narrative.

In the quietude of solitude, we revisit these stories. Some bring a smile, a slight curve on the lips. Others, a furrow in the brow. They're omnipresent, these narratives, coloring our solace with the shades of our lived experiences.

Consider the power of revising these narratives. It's a daunting task, akin to editing the script of one's life while the play is live. But it's possible. The stories we tell ourselves about who we are, they're not etched in stone. They're written in the sand, at the edge where consciousness meets the sea of change.

Some narratives serve. They propel us forward, instill resilience. Others constrain, bind us to past versions of ourselves that no longer exist. The art lies in discerning which narratives to carry forward, and which to let float away with the tides of time.

Rewriting is a process. It starts with awareness, a beacon in the fog. Realizing that the narrative is, in fact, a narrative and not an immutable fact. It's about seeing the authorship we hold, the pen that's been in our hands all along.

We seek coherence in our narratives, even when life offers none. The mind abhors a vacuum. It fills the gaps, sometimes with fiction. It's a peculiar aspect of the human condition, this need to make sense of what is, more often than not, senseless.

The narratives of loss and trauma are the heaviest to carry. They shape us in profound ways, cutting grooves into our very essence. Here lies the greatest challenge and the greatest opportunity for rewriting. It's about finding meaning, a semblance of understanding, in the caverns of pain.

Our narratives intersect. They don't exist in isolation. They're influenced by the stories of those around us, a communal fabric of sorts. It's in the sharing that healing often begins, where understanding broadens, where narratives find their echo in the other.

Professional narratives are peculiar. They often follow a script society hands us. Climbing ladders, ticking boxes. Yet, beneath the surface, there exists a narrative more personal, more authentic. It's about daring to redefine success, on terms that resonate with the inner self.

As we age, the narrative evolves. It's supposed to. With each decade, the story grows. It becomes richer, layered. What was important once may no longer hold sway. It's a sign of growth, of life lived in its multifaceted complexity.

In the end, our narratives are all we have. They're the legacy we leave behind, the stories etched into the hearts and minds of those we touched. It's about crafting these narratives with intention, with mindfulness, with an awareness of the fleeting beauty that is life.

Forgetting and Remaking the Self

We forget. It's what we do, consciously or not. Wrapped up in the day-to-day, memories fade. Who we were ten, twenty, or thirty years ago dissolves. And in that forgetting, room emerges. Space for rebirth. The self is not static. It morphs; influenced by every breath, every interaction.

Imagine the self as a house. Over time, rooms clutter with memories, beliefs, and identities. Sometimes, it's necessary to clear out. To forget. To demolish the old, making way for the new. This is the essence of remaking the self. It's not about discarding who we are but understanding that growth requires letting go.

Forgetting is often viewed negatively. A loss. But what if it's a gift? A chance to unlearn the conditioning of our minds. Every forgotten piece is an opportunity to question, "Who am I without this?" It's in the spaces of not knowing that we find room to explore, to stretch into new shapes.

Who told you who you should be? The roles we play, the expectations we meet, they're scripts written by society, family, friends. They're not inherently ours. Forgetting those parts of our self-scripted by others allows us to author our own existence.

Think about beliefs. How many do you carry that were never truly yours? Forgetting these, intentionally setting them aside, opens a canvas. Now, what do you paint? What colors do you choose when the palette is no longer limited by past shades?

Remaking the self is an art. It's the conscious decision to sculpt your being into forms that fit who you are now, not who you were. It requires courage. Forgetting is not for the faint of heart. It demands we confront the void, the unknown. Yet, isn't there beauty in creation? In deciding, moment by moment, who you wish to be?

Much of our pain comes from clinging. To past hurts, to outdated versions of ourselves. Pain thrives in stagnation. But when we allow forgetting, we make peace with impermanence. We learn to dance in the changing tides of identity, embracing each wave of becoming with open arms.

And so, we gather the courage to forget. To let go of the narratives that no longer serve us. In their place, we craft new stories. Stories of who we are becoming.

This doesn't mean dismissing the past entirely; it means not allowing it to dictate our future. We honor our history by transforming it.

Imagine standing at a crossroads. Behind you, a path well-traveled, lined with the echoes of your past selves. Ahead, the road is unpaved, unknown. Remaking the self begins with a step into that uncertainty. With each step, the path develops, shaped by present desires, dreams, and the sheer will to explore.

Our society praises the known, the secure. But is there not freedom in forgetting? In the release of past weights, do we not learn to fly? Embrace the liberation of remaking, the joy found in discovering facets of yourself you never knew existed. It's a journey of endless horizons, of self in perpetual rebirth.

Forgetting the self is as natural as the changing seasons. Each fall, leaves are shed, trees stand bare. Yet, come spring, they blossom anew. So too, must we allow ourselves to shed old identities, to endure periods of bareness, knowing that with time, new aspects of ourselves will blossom.

This remaking isn't a solitary process. We are mirrors, reflecting and being reflected by those around us. The self is remade not just internally but through our interactions, our relationships. Each person we meet, every experience, leaves a mark, softly sculpting us into new beings.

But caution is needed. Forgetting and remaking don't mean discarding the core, the essence of who you are. It's about refinement, shedding layers to reveal more of your true self. It's the delicate balance between holding on and letting go, between past lessons and present growth.

So we walk this earth, forgetting, remaking. Each day a chance to redefine. What will you forget today? What will you become tomorrow? The self is a masterpiece, never finished, always in the making.

Chapter 9:
The Philosophy of Self

Life, at its core, asks of us, "Who am I?" This question, timeless in its persistence, threads through the fabric of our existence, weaving patterns of thought that stretch from the ancient hills of the East to the busy streets of the West. We stand, often in silence, grappling with this existential anchor, finding our reflections in the still waters of thought. The philosophy of self isn't just a topic; it's a journey, one that digs deep into the soil of our being, unearthing the roots of what it means to truly exist. Western perspectives armor us with the sword of individualism, casting the self as a fortress to be fortified and defended. Yet, in the East, the self flows like water, an entity less defined by boundaries and more by its place within the cosmos. We've come to understand the self not as a singular, but as a multitude, a convergence of many streams. The search for purpose then becomes not a quest for a definitive answer but a journey of understanding the layers that compose us. In our contemplation, we find that the philosophy of self is not a static study but a living, breathing dialogue with our innermost beings. It's a dialogue that enriches us, challenges us, and ultimately, shapes the very essence of our being.

Existential Questions

When we unhinge the door to the philosophy of self, it swings open to a room filled with existential questions. At its heart, the voice that whispers, "Who am I?" This question, simple yet profound, drives us into the labyrinth of our own existence. It's not about the reflection in the mirror but what flickers behind those eyes. In the everyday rush, we rarely stop to ponder this. Yet, the question hovers, a shadow trailing our steps. The search for purpose adds layers to this quest. It's a terrain where purpose isn't handed down but forged by our hands, in the decisions we make, the paths we choose, and the ones we walk away from. It's a dialogue, not just with the self but with the universe. What are we but a speck in the vastness, yet a speck that yearns to understand its place? Here, the philosophy of self doesn't offer answers but instead sharpens our questions, reminding us that to ask, to search, is perhaps to be truly alive.

"Who am I?"

This question sits at the heart of every venture into the self. A question so simple in its asking, yet vast in its implications. We start from what we know, or what we think we know, and peel back layers, hoping to find a core truth. But is there such a core? Or are we, in fact, an amalgamation of experiences, thoughts, beliefs, and the sheer accident of our births? Let's explore.

We've learned about the brain, about society's role, about the emotional currents that steer us. Yet, when we turn inward to ask, "Who am I?" do these faculties offer clarity, or do they further obscure our view? It seems the closer we look, the more complex the picture becomes.

Consider the physical self first. It's tangible, measurable. You can catalog your features, your DNA, your brain patterns. But are you just the sum of these parts? Or is there something ineffable, something beyond the physical that defines you?

Then there's the mental self. Your thoughts, your intelligence. But thoughts shift, evolve. Can a fleeting thought capture the essence of who you are? It's like trying to hold water in your hands. The more tightly you grasp, the less you hold.

The spiritual aspect then whispers for attention. It's the hardest to define, rooted in feelings and beliefs rather than concrete evidence. Here, in the quiet spaces of the mind, the question "Who am I?" resonates most deeply.

Reading through historical and modern interpretations, it's clear we're not the first to grapple with this question. It's a quest that has consumed philosophers, scientists, and seekers for centuries. Is there a definitive answer? Or is the essence of the self something that constantly evolves?

Our surroundings shape us. Society, with its norms and traditions, presses us into molds. Some fit snugly; others chafe. The social self is a dancer, constantly moving in tune with or against the rhythm of societal expectations. Yet, can the self be distilled to how well you navigate societal norms?

Emotionally, we're an ocean. Calm and raging in turns. Emotions color every aspect of our being, yet they're ephemeral. Joy, sorrow, love, anger - they pass through us, leaving their mark. Can the essence of who we are be captured in these fleeting hues?

Consider the roles you play. Professional, friend, lover, enemy. Each role demands a different you. Is the self merely a chameleon, changing color to match its surroundings? And if so, does the chameleon have a true color of its own?

Memory plays tricks on us. It edits, distorts, omits. Our personal narrative is a story we tell ourselves, but how true is it? If our memories shape our sense of self, and our memories are flawed, what does that say about our understanding of ourselves?

In the philosophy of self, we're encouraged to peel back these layers. But with each layer removed, we don't find simple answers. Instead, we uncover more questions. The quest for the self is not a journey with a clear destination but a perpetual exploration.

Spirituality offers a different lens. Here, the question of "Who am I?" is not about distinguishing oneself from others but about finding unity. It's seeing the self as a drop in an endless ocean, significant not in its separateness but in its part of the whole.

As we change, grow, adapt, the self too is in flux. What defined you a decade ago, a year ago, even yesterday, may not hold true today. The self is not a static entity but a dynamic, evolving construct.

In the digital realm, we craft avatars, curate online personas. Another layer of the self, but one that raises its own questions. Is this digital self a true reflection of who we are, or another mask we wear?

So, "Who am I?" Perhaps it's the wrong question. Perhaps the question isn't about finding a definitive answer but about learning to live with the mystery. To embrace the multitude within, to recognize that we are, at every moment, both everything and nothing at all.

The Search for Purpose

It's a journey each of us take. Starts early or late, depends. We're born, we grow, we question. Jobs. Relationships. We're looking for meaning in them. Sometimes, it feels like we're walking in circles. We ask, "Why am I here?" It's life. It's how it unfolds.

Life doesn't come with an instruction manual. Wish it did. It gives us choices though, lots of them. Each choice paves a path. Some lead to dead ends, others to vistas unseen. The purpose? It's not hanging on a signpost. It's buried. In actions, feelings, the lives we touch.

Modern life. It's busy. Got our heads down, always pushing. Gotta stop. Look around. The meaning, the purpose we chase - it's not out in the world. It's in us. It's what we make of what we've got. The challenges, the triumphs, they sculpt us.

Think. Real hard. What drives you? Money? Recognition? These are sand. They slip right through when you grasp too tight. Something sturdier is needed. Love. Passion. A cause. Something that stands when the storm hits.

But how to find it, that's the question. Some look outside. Travel. Adventure. It's good, opens the eyes. But the real journey? It's inward. In the silent spaces of the mind, that's where purpose whispers.

It's easy to get lost. Society shouts, tells us what we need to be happy. A nice house. A flashy car. It's noise. Distracts us from what's essential. The search for purpose is personal. Can't be handed to you. You've got to dig for it. Through the layers of should and must. Until you find the want. The need.

Failure. It's part of the journey. We stumble. We fall. But we learn. Every misstep brings us closer. It reveals a piece of the puzzle. The image it forms? That's for you to decide. But it's there, in the tapestry of trials and errors.

Connection. Don't underestimate it. Sometimes our purpose is reflected in others. In helping, in teaching, in loving. It's a mirror. Shows us who we are, what we're meant to do. But it requires us to look, really look.

And the mind, it's a tool. Powerful. Shapes our reality. Our thoughts, they're seeds. Plant them with care. Negativity, doubt, they choke the life out of purpose. Positive, nurturing thoughts? They let it bloom.

Time doesn't wait. Slips through our fingers like water. Each moment is a chance. A choice. To live with purpose or to drift. Drifting's easy. It's the current of life. Living with purpose? That's swimming against the tide. Hard. But rewarding.

Age. It's just a number. Purpose doesn't care if you're 20 or 50. It's never too late. Never too early. Starts when you decide. Take the step. Use what you've learned. Your experiences. They're your compass.

Simplicity. There's beauty in it. Purpose doesn't have to be grand. It's not about moving mountains. Sometimes, it's in the small things. A smile. A kind word. Changing one life for the better. That's purpose too.

It's a quest. Never really ends. We evolve, our purpose shifts. What mattered at 20 might not at 40. And that's okay. It's part of the journey. Discovering, rediscovering who we are, what we're here for.

Patience. It's key. Purpose doesn't reveal itself overnight. It's a slow dance. Two steps forward, one step back. But with each move, the picture clears. The path reveals itself. And when it does, it's like the sun breaking through after a storm. Illuminating.

Finally, remember. The search for purpose, it's uniquely yours. Can't be compared, can't be measured.

It's a journey of a thousand steps. A journey worth taking. So take it. Find your purpose. Live it. It's the most precious thing you've got.

Eastern vs. Western Perspectives

The philosophy of self weaves a vibrant tapestry across cultures. It stretches, twines, and intertwines from East to West, each thread colored with its own perception of what it means to truly be. There's rhythm in this difference, a balance that's often hard to grasp. Eastern and Western philosophies, at their core, propose distinctive viewpoints, yet they are in perpetual conversation about the essence of the self. This discourse bridges oceans, traditions, generations. It's complex. It's layered. It's rich.

Western thought often prides itself on the individual. The spotlight shines on personal achievements, rights, freedoms. It's the soil where the "I" flourishes. You've felt it, right? The urge to stand out, to be seen uniquely. It's in the air we breathe in the West. A narrative deeply ingrained, pushing one towards a distinct identity, separate from the crowd. In this narrative, the self is an autonomous entity, steering its own course through the waters of life.

Turn your gaze Eastward, though, and you'll notice a shift. The self melds with community, tradition, collective. Here, identity is often about harmonizing with the larger group, not standing apart. It's about continuity, a seamless thread in the fabric of a broader, more intricate design. In Eastern philosophy, the self isn't an island but a bridge connecting people, places, ideas.

Consider the Buddhist notion of no-self, or Anatta. It challenges the very foundation of what many in the West take for granted: the existence of a permanent, unchanging self. Instead, it presents us with a self that's fluid, transient, ever-changing through the flow of experiences. It's a thought that might unsettle or liberate, depending on how you see it.

Then there's the Confucian emphasis on roles, responsibilities, and relationships. It's a dance of duties, where the self is defined much by its place in the web of social interactions. This isn't about erosion of identity but fulfillment through a meticulously crafted social harmony.

In contrast, the Western canon, with its ancient Greek roots, speaks of virtues, individuality, and personal excellence. The Platonic and Aristotelian legacies emphasize a form of self-cultivation too, but there's a striking difference. It's more about polishing one's own stone rather than fitting it into an elaborate mosaic.

The dialogue between these perspectives isn't one of opposition but complementarity. Think of it as a spectrum. Where do we find ourselves along this stretch? It's a question worth pondering. Because life—our work, relationships, innermost feelings—is often about navigating this spectrum, sometimes leaning a little to one side, sometimes to the other.

Implications stretch far and wide, from how we perceive success to how we face adversity. In a Western framework, success is often personalized—my achievement, my victory. Adversity, similarly, is a personal challenge to overcome, a testament to individual resilience.

Eastern perspectives offer a different lens. Success is communal, a shared joy. Adversity, then, becomes a collective hurdle, something to be faced with the support of the community, a reminder of interconnectedness.

In the realm of the workplace, these perspectives impact leadership styles, decision-making, team dynamics. The Western model often emphasizes leadership as a showcase of personal excellence and decisiveness. Eastern models might stress consensus, collective input.

But it's not all black and white. Cultures merge, philosophies evolve. The global village blurs these distinctions, creating spaces where Eastern and Western thoughts meet, meld, and sometimes clash. It's fascinating, sometimes messy, often enriching.

Personal development, then, can be seen through this prism of cultural philosophy. What aspects of the self are we nurturing? Are we seeking personal acclaim, or finding our purpose within the community? How do we balance these drives? There's no one-size-fits-all answer, but the journey is profoundly personal and universally human.

As working professionals, navigating this landscape can be daunting. Marketplaces are increasingly global, workplaces more diverse. We're asked to juggle these philosophies daily. To be individual yet team players, autonomous yet interconnected.

In our interactions, our leadership, our pursuit of happiness, knowing where these philosophies overlap, and where they diverge, equips us with a map. It helps us understand not just others but ourselves, in a world that's often too busy to ponder the question of the self.

So, as we tread our paths, let's remember the richness of these perspectives. They offer us not just a way to view the self but a myriad of lenses through which we can understand the world. And in understanding, perhaps, we find ways to bridge the gap, to navigate the wonderful, wide spectrum of the human experience.

Chapter 10: Spirituality and the Sense of Self

Spirituality shapes us. It's like water, flowing around the edges of our being, carving out caverns of belief and pools of faith in its wake. We tread through life, sometimes aware, often not, of how profoundly this undercurrent affects our identity. In it, the spiritual self is more than an abstract concept; it is a tangible presence that interacts with our everyday lives, shaping our decisions, our values, and our understanding of who we are in the vast, interconnected web of existence. It's quiet, this influence, yet persistent, echoing in the chambers of the heart and mind with each breath, each moment of stillness, each instance of awe in the face of the divine or the Universe.

The dialogue between spirituality and self is an ancient one, stretching back to the dawn of consciousness, perhaps. It speaks to the core of our being, asking us to consider not just who we are, but why we are. This chapter delves into that dialogue, exploring how spiritual practices and beliefs, from

115

mindfulness to meditation, from the doctrines of age-old religions to the quiet, personal quests for meaning, shape the fabric of our selfhood. It's in the silent moments, in the depth of meditation or prayer, that many find a connection to something greater than themselves, a sense of unity and belonging that transcends the individual and reaches for the universal.

Yet, this journey is deeply personal, as varied as the lives of those who walk the earth. It's a path that cuts through the noise of daily life, leading us to moments of clarity and understanding that redefine our place in the world. As we peel back the layers of social expectation, professional identity, and the roles we play, we get closer to the essence of our true self, illuminated by the spiritual beliefs that resonate with our innermost being. This exploration isn't merely academic; it's a necessary pilgrimage to understand the self in its most profound sense. How does spirituality inform our sense of self? It does so by bridging the finite and the infinite, grounding us in the present while inviting us to ponder the eternal.

Exploring Spiritual Dimensions

In the terrain of spirituality, we delve beyond the hard surface of the empirical, venturing into the soft soil of the subjective. Here, memory and identity converge beneath a broader expanse, one not solely defined by the physical or the cognitive, but by a connection to something transcendent. This transcendent connection, varying widely among individuals, roots us in a sense of purpose larger than the self. It whispers of ancient traditions and modern practices that seek not to answer but to question, 'what is it that truly connects us?' In this exploration, the concept of self expands, reaching into realms unseen, unmeasured, untouched by the tools of science, yet profoundly felt. It's a journey inward, and yet, outward—a paradox that speaks to the essence of being human. It's here, amidst these spiritual dimensions, that many find anchors in the storm, sails for the windless days, navigational stars by which to chart a course through the often tumultuous seas of life. This section isn't just about religion or meditation; it's an invitation to look beyond the horizon of the known into the vast, uncharted waters of spiritual consciousness.

Religious Traditions

It's dark outside. Inside, a single flame flickers. It's always been this way. Since time immemorial, humans have sought to understand their place in the vast expanse of the universe. They looked at the stars, at the vast deserts, the endless seas, and they wondered. They asked the night sky, the wind, the thundering rivers. Who are we?

These questions found their first answers in stories. Myths. Legends. Gods and demons. Heaven and hell. Rebirth and liberation. These aren't just tales. They're the scaffolding of civilizations, the framework of cultures. And at the heart of these narratives are the religious traditions that have shaped, and been shaped by, the human quest for meaning.

In the silence of a monastery, a monk sits in meditation. His mind, they say, touches a silence so profound that words fail to capture its essence. This pursuit of inner peace, of enlightenment, is a thread that runs through many religious traditions. It's an acknowledgment that the self is both a mystery and a revelation, a question and an answer.

In the bustling streets of a city halfway across the world, a call to prayer echoes. It's a reminder, five times a day, of submission to a higher power, of belonging to a community that spans continents. Islam, with its emphasis on the Ummah, the community of believers, speaks to the social aspect of the self. It's a narrative of unity, of finding oneself in the collective, in the shared practices, in the fasting and the feasts.

Turn the pages of ancient texts. The Bhagavad Gita, for example, is a dialogue between prince Arjuna and Lord Krishna on the battlefield. It's a profound exploration of duty, righteousness, and the nature of the self. "You are your own friend," says Krishna, "and you are your own enemy." Here, in this epic, is the understanding that the self is a battleground of moral choices, a journey of spiritual growth.

In the quiet of a synagogue, the reading of the Torah unfolds. The stories of Abraham, Isaac, Jacob, and Moses aren't just historical narratives; they're moral and spiritual blueprints. Judaism emphasizes the covenant, the law, and the pursuit of justice and compassion. It teaches that the self is realized not in isolation but in community, in the shared memories and hopes of a people.

Then there are the great cycles of nature that indigenous religions celebrate; the rhythms of the earth and the sky, the cycle of life and death. Here, the self is not apart from nature but a part of nature. It's a perspective that enriches the conversation about the self, reminding us of our interconnection with the world around us.

And let's not forget the revolution that was Christianity. In a time of empires, it spoke to the heart of the individual. "The kingdom of God is within you," Jesus said. It was a radical invitation to find divinity not in the marble statues of the gods but within the human heart. It's a narrative that emphasizes love, forgiveness, and personal transformation.

Across the oceans, in the great plains and forests of America, the Native American spiritual traditions saw the divine in the eagle's flight, the buffalo's path, and the flow of the river. Theirs was a spirituality that acknowledged the sacred in the natural, in the communal dance, in the vision quest. Here, the self is a part of a larger story, a story of harmony and respect.

Each of these traditions, and countless others, hold a piece of the puzzle that is the self. They offer narratives of creation and destruction, of exile and return, of suffering and redemption. They speak to the many facets of the human experience: our fears and hopes, our joys and sorrows.

But it's not just about the narratives or the rituals, the prayers or the meditations. It's about the questions these traditions invite us to ask. Who am I? What is my purpose? How do I find peace, justice, love? These aren't abstract philosophical queries; they're the most practical questions of our lives. They're about the everyday choices we make, the relationships we nurture, the kind of people we choose to become.

So, as we sit at our desks, in our homes, or on a park bench, these traditions whisper to us. They remind us that the search for the self is perhaps the oldest and most shared quest of humanity. They tell us that we're not alone in our doubts and our longings, in our joys and our sorrows.

Yes, the world has changed. We live in an age of science and technology, of social media and artificial intelligence. But the fundamental questions remain. And the religious traditions, with their rich tapesties of beliefs, practices, and narratives, continue to offer insights into the nature of the self, into the art of living a meaningful life.

In the end, it's about dialogue. A conversation between the past and the present, the ancient and the modern. It's a conversation that invites us to listen, to reflect, and to grow. It's a journey into the heart of what it means to be human, a journey that each of us must undertake for ourselves. But within the stories and practices of these religious traditions, we find companions for the journey. Guides. Lights in the darkness. Echoes of our shared quest for understanding, for peace, for home.

So we listen. We learn. And, slowly, we begin to understand the contours of the self, to unravel the conditioning of our own minds. It's a path that leads us not just outward into the world but inward, into the deepest parts of ourselves. And there, in the quiet and the stillness, we might just find the answers we've been seeking.

Mindfulness and Meditation

The morning starts not with coffee, but with silence. The day's first task isn't a check of emails, but a checking-in with oneself. In the realm of mindfulness and meditation, this isn't just a practice, it's a gateway. A gateway that no bustling schedule can afford to ignore any longer.

Consider the mind as a vast, often tumultuous sea. Waves of thoughts, storms of emotions. Now imagine finding a calm amidst this. Not by ceasing the storm, but by observing it. This is mindfulness. A simple, yet profound act of being present. In the workplace, amidst deadlines and demands, mindfulness becomes an anchor.

Meditation, its close kin, takes this present-mindedness further. It's the deliberate practice of focus, an invitation to quiet the mental chatter. Many think it demands hours, cross-legged under Bodhi trees. It doesn't. Just minutes can carve pathways in the brain, a fact modern neuroscience nods to.

Why this matters to the working professional spans several reasons. Stress, the age-old adversary in the corporate arena, is one. Mindfulness and meditation don't erase stress, but they change how one interacts with it. Less reactivity, more reflection.

The day breaks with decisions. Some trivial, some monumental. Clarity often gets clouded under pressure. Enter meditation. It cultivates a space, allowing thoughts to pass without getting ensnared. What emerges is clarity, an invaluable asset in decision making.

Then there's creativity, a muscle that thrives not on the constant noise but on moments of silence. Mindfulness fosters an environment where creativity isn't just welcomed; it's nurtured.

The narrative of the self, too, finds its chapters rewritten in the quiet. Beyond the roles and titles, beneath the accomplishments, who is the 'I' that shows up to work each day? Meditation offers a mirror, reflecting a self unencumbered by identities.

Communication, often littered with misunderstandings, benefits as well. Mindfulness teaches listening, not just hearing. It cultivates empathy by encouraging a moment's pause to truly understand another's perspective. In a world quick to speak, this is a rare treasure.

Leadership, too, transforms. A leader imbued with mindfulness and meditation leads not from a pedestal, but from amongst. They embody patience and radiate calm, becoming beacons in turbulent times.

Consider the professional at their desk, the weight of the day pressing down. They pause, breathe, and practice a moment of mindfulness. This isn't time lost. It's an investment. An investment in a mind that returns to the task more focused, more grounded.

This practice isn't a diversion from productivity; it's an enhancer. Studies underscore it, tales of transformation champion it. Yet, skepticism lingers, a remnant of a culture enamored with unceasing productivity. But what if true productivity isn't measured in tasks completed, but in clarity gained, in stress abated, in creativity unleashed?

The path of mindfulness and meditation doesn't demand detachment from worldly affairs. It asks for engagement with the present. It teaches that amid the cacophony of deadlines, meetings, and expectations, there exists a quietude within. A quietude that isn't just peace, but power.

The day winds down. The professional looks back, not just on tasks completed, but on moments of presence, of mindful engagement with themselves and their work. They've not just worked; they've woven mindfulness into the fabric of their day.

And so, the exploration of mindfulness and meditation isn't merely an exercise for the personal sphere. It's an essential for the professional. It's a reorientation of the self in the world of work, a rediscovery of the essence of being in the midst of doing. In the narrative of self-discovery, mindfulness and meditation emerge not just as chapters, but as guiding principles, leading one towards a self that isn't just productive, but peaceful, purposeful, and profoundly present.

Chapter 11:
The Changing Self

Change, they say, is the only constant. Amidst the tangles of our routines, the self is a ship navigating through storms and calm alike. It's about adaptation and growth, each moment a carpenter's tool shaping the hull, each decision a gust against the sails. Life doesn't hand us a map. It throws transitions our way - jobs lost, loves found, dreams traded for new horizons. We're resilient, though. Like cities rebuilt on the ruins of their past, we find strength in our foundations, discovering that reinvention is not the erasure of yesterday but the embracing of tomorrow. Here in the flux, amidst life's ceaseless churn, the self finds its true form. Not static, but dynamic. Not imprisoned in yesterday's shell, but always molding in the kiln of experience. This chapter isn't just a reflection on change; it's a guide through the wilderness of self-transformation, where every step forward is a testament to our undying capacity for rebirth.

Adaptation and Growth

Change is the only constant; it's the heart of growth, beating strong, pushing us into the unknown. In our lives, transitions are inevitable. We move, change jobs, relationships evolve or end. Each shift demands adaptation, a remolding of the self that's both terrifying and exhilarating. It's in these moments, standing at the precipice of the familiar and the new, that we truly understand the capacity of the human spirit to adapt. Growth isn't just about expansion, reaching up towards the sky; it's about depth, digging into the dark soil of our experiences, finding nutrients in the murk. Resilience isn't born from the absence of struggle but is forged in the relentless pursuit of moving forward, even when the path is obscured. Reinvention, then, isn't an act of becoming something entirely new but remembering who we were meant to be before the world told us who to be. Each adaptation, each growth spurt, is a return, a homecoming to a self that exists beyond the layers of societal expectations and self-imposed limitations. And as we navigate through life's transitions, we find that growth is not just about changing who we are but about shedding who we are not, revealing the unblemished truth that rests within.

Life Transitions

Change. Inevitable. Comes like the tide, yet we stand at the shore, hoping to hold it at bay with nothing but our will. Life transitions are the embodiment of this paradox. We grow, we evolve, we change. From college to first job. From a singleton to a partner in the dance of life. From carefree youth to responsible adulthood. Each transition whispers of the self, morphing, adapting, yet ever constant.

It's in the moments of transition that we find ourselves at the crossroads. The job lost or left behind, the marriage begun or ended, the move across town or across the world. These aren't just changes. They are rebirths. Each transition, a shedding of an old skin. What remains is the core of our being, yet how often do we recognize this amidst the tumult of change?

There's a simplicity in the complex nature of transitions. Like the changing seasons, they follow a pattern, a cycle. And yet, no two transitions are quite the same. The profundity of these moments can't be understated. They sculpt us, painstakingly, into who we are meant to become.

Think of the young professional, stepping into their first major role. The weight of expectation, the thrill of potential. It's a transition that is both a beginning and an end. The end of what was known and comfortable, the beginning of a journey into the self. Who am I in this new role? Can I shape this role to better fit the contours of my true self?

And then, consider the transition to parenthood. Nothing quite epitomizes life's transitions like it. Here, the self is both diminished and magnified. Time once your own is now overwhelmingly occupied by another, and yet, in this shift, a new depth of self-understanding is unearthed.

Transitions force us to confront the question of authenticity. In adapting to our new roles, do we lose a piece of ourselves or do we uncover a more genuine aspect of our being that lay dormant? The challenge lies not in the transition itself but in our response to it. Do we resist, clinging to the familiar past, or do we embrace, allowing the unfamiliar to transform us?

It's said that in every ending there is a beginning. This is the essence of transitions. They are not merely points of change but are, in themselves, processes. Processes of letting go, of beginning anew, of learning and unlearning. They remind us that the self is not static but fluid, always in the process of becoming.

In the world of work and career, transitions hold a special significance. The professional self is in constant negotiation between personal aspirations and the demands of the job. A promotion, a shift in career, or even retirement, each represents a negotiation of identity, a reevaluation of the self in the light of new circumstances.

Consider also the transitions that are not chosen but thrust upon us. Illness, bereavement, the unforeseen events that alter the course of our lives in ways we hadn't imagined. Here, the self is tested, resilience is built, and the depth of our inner resources is revealed.

There's beauty in these transitions, in the impermanence they represent. Like the Zen practice of creating intricate sand mandalas only to let them be swept away, life transitions teach us the art of attachment and detachment, of investing ourselves fully in the moment and yet not losing ourselves when the moment passes.

The self, then, is not a fixed entity but a narrative in constant flux. Life's transitions are the chapters of this narrative, each transition a turning point, a plot twist leading us to unforeseen developmental arcs.

Bringing consciousness to these transitions allows us to navigate them with grace. It is not about controlling the change but about engaging with it, allowing it to unfold, and finding our place within it. It requires a mindfulness, an openness to experience, and a willingness to learn.

At its core, each transition holds a lesson. It's a teacher, albeit a harsh one at times. The lessons learned are not just about the self but also about the world around us. They teach us empathy, resilience, and the power of renewal.

In conclusion, life transitions are not merely changes to be endured but opportunities for growth and self-discovery. They are the crucibles in which our true selves are forged. By embracing them, we embrace the fullness of life and the endless possibilities for becoming that life offers.

Resilience and Reinvention

Life molds us. Each sunrise and sunset marks a new chance, or so we like to think. But what about the chances that slip by? As working professionals, we hustle. We're told every moment is an opportunity. Yet, in the scramble, parts of us get lost, worn out, or overlooked. So, we adapt. We grow resilient. We reinvent. But is it as straightforward as it appears?

Understand this: Resilience isn't merely bouncing back. It's deeper. It's about wrestling with the storms life hurls at us and still moving forward. It's about the capacity to endure loss, setbacks, failures, and transforming these into a driving force.

Reinvention, then, is the sibling of resilience. A quiet, potent force. It whispers in our failures, our losses, and in the dead of night. It asks, "Is this the person you wish to be?" Rarely do we have an immediate answer. And that's okay. Reinvention doesn't demand haste. It demands honesty.

The process is as personal as it gets. There's no universal blueprint, no one-size-fits-all. What worked for one might not for another. This journey towards resilience and reinvention is a solitary path, paved with introspection, self-awareness, and the courage to confront our deepest fears and flaws.

Reflection is our tool, our weapon. It's looking in the mirror and seeing beyond the physical. It's understanding that every scar, every wrinkle, every smile line tells a story. The story of resilience. Our narratives are rich with reinvention, even if we fail to recognize it.

Let's talk about the setbacks. The moments when everything crumbles, and hope seems like a distant memory. Here, resilience is our foundation. Without it, reinvention is a castle built on sand. Shaky. Unsustainable. To reinvent is to believe in the possibility of change, both internal and external. It's to believe in tomorrow, even when today is heavy with despair.

Consider the role of failure in this process. Society teaches us to fear failure, to avoid it at all costs. But what if we embraced it instead? What if we viewed each failure as a step towards reinvention? Failure is not the opposite of success; it's a vital component of it. Failures are not setbacks; they're redirections, guiding us towards a version of ourselves we've yet to become.

Think about the growth mindset. It's this perspective that allows resilience to flourish. It's believing that effort can lead to mastery, that challenges are opportunities to grow. This mindset is key in the reinvention process. Without it, we remain stuck, unable to evolve beyond our current selves.

Adaptation then comes into play. Much like how species evolve to survive, we too must adapt to our changing environments, roles, and identities. Adaptation is how we survive. But to thrive? That requires resilience and the willingness to reinvent.

Now, consider the encounters that shape us. The people we meet, the experiences we undergo, the mistakes we make. Each one has the potential to alter the trajectory of our lives. This is where resilience is tested, and reinvention is born. It's in these moments that we decide who we want to be, independent of who we were.

The question then becomes, how do we foster resilience? It starts with self-care. Not the superficial kind, but the kind that nourishes our soul, sharpens our mind, and strengthens our body. It's about setting boundaries, acknowledging our needs, and realizing that it's okay to put ourselves first.

And what of reinvention? It begins with a question. A simple yet profound one: Who do I want to be? This question is the seed from which the journey of reinvention grows. It's about envisioning a future self and taking concrete steps towards becoming that person. It's about not being afraid to let go of outdated identities, beliefs, or habits that no longer serve us.

The path toward resilience and reinvention is fraught with challenges, yes. It's a path that demands everything we've got and then some. But it's also a path that leads to growth, discovery, and, ultimately, a deeper understanding and appreciation of the self. This journey is not for the faint of heart. Yet, it is perhaps the most rewarding journey one can undertake.

In the end, resilience and reinvention are about embracing change. It's about recognizing that change is the only constant in life and learning to dance with it. It's a continuous process, a cycle of evolving and becoming. As working professionals between 20 to 50, our time is now. The question is, are we ready to meet ourselves anew?

Chapter 12:
The Digital Self

In the fabric of today's existence, pixels and code intertwine with flesh and bone, crafting a new layer to our being: the digital self. We navigate this realm, sometimes with more agility and understanding than our physical world. It shapes us, molds our perceptions, influences our interactions. Here, identity is fluid, constantly reshaped by the streams of data we dive into daily. Yet, it's easy to overlook how deeply this digital existence infiltrates our sense of self, how it expands our reach yet confines us in frames of likes, shares, and fleeting attention. The screens serve as both windows and mirrors, reflecting fragmented versions of ourselves, pieced together through curated galleries and snippets of character-limited thoughts. This chapter delves into the essence of our online identities, exploring the impact of technology on our self-perception and social connections. It questions the authenticity of our digital expressions and ponders the future of personal identity in an increasingly virtual world. Amidst this exploration, we find ourselves at a crossroads between embracing the boundless potential of digital evolution and preserving the core that makes us uniquely human. The balance is delicate, yet crucial, as we forge ahead into the uncharted territories of the digital age.

The Impact of Technology

Technology threads through our lives, unasked yet omnipresent, shaping thoughts and dreams, molding who we are in bits and pixels. It's a silent river, carving canyons in the landscape of the self. We tap and swipe, crafting identities with each online interaction. The lines blur. Where does the digital self end and the flesh-and-blood self begin? In this age, we are architects of digital avatars, curating lives on screens, yet the essence, the core of who we are, remains a question mark, an enigma drowned out by the constant hum of the digital age. It's seductive, this power to craft oneself anew, to break free from the physical confines and explore identities in spaces where rules of the tangible world don't apply. Yet, in this freedom, there's a tether. Technology, for all its promises of connection, often isolates, leaving us adrift among a sea of faces glowing in the dark, each lost in their own digital reflection. We're left to wonder, in this web of interconnected selves, where do we truly find connection, understanding, the touchstone of reality?

It's a dance of shadows and light, the digital self, a facet of who we are, yet never the sum total. As we navigate this new terrain, the impact of technology on the self is profound, redefining boundaries, possibilities, and the very essence of what it means to know oneself.

Online Identity

It swims in digital streams. It lives in bytes and pixels. Our online self, a reflection or maybe a distortion. Who can tell anymore? The screen blinks. We type. We share. We exist. Somehow different yet the same.

We were once confined to the flesh, to the immediate circle of friends, family, colleagues. Our voices, our stories, could only travel as far as our physical selves could take them. But now? We project our voices across the globe. Our thoughts, once intimate and personal, are broadcast for any and all to see. We are authors of our digital selves, curating the images and words that present us to the online world.

Our online identity. It's tricky. A mask? A truth? It's both. We put forward the best, or sometimes the worst, depending on the shadow or light we stand in at the moment. Our profiles, a gallery. Pictures. Texts. Endless scrolls of our digital footprints. They say, "This is me. But, also, maybe, it's who I want you to think I am." The distinction blurs.

Consider the power, the sheer magnitude of being able to connect with anyone, anywhere, at any time. Our grandparents couldn't fathom it. Our parents stumbled into it. We plunge into it, sometimes headfirst, without looking. We swipe. We click. We like. In doing so, we build bridges. But also walls.

Each post, each tweet, each photo shared, is a brick in the wall of our online identity. Carefully placed. Sometimes impulsively slapped together. It shapes how others see us, but also how we see ourselves. The digital mirror is unrelenting, always there, asking us to stare into it, to judge, to compare.

What happens when the line between our online self and our real-world self begins to blur? When the accolades we receive online start to mean more than the warmth of a human touch or the genuine laugh shared in a coffee shop? There's a danger there. A loss of touch. The digital self, while powerful, while freeing, can also cage us.

We chase likes, comments, shares. Validation comes not from within, but from the ever-changing algorithm of social approval. Our worth, quantified by notifications. It's addictive. It's unsettling. Our online identity, while offering a form of expression, can also trap us in a perpetual cycle of seeking external validation.

Yet, there's beauty here too. In the connections. In the finding of like-minded souls across continents who whisper, "You are not alone." Our online identity can be a beacon, a signal flare sent up into the digital night sky, saying, "Here I am. Here is my truth." It's powerful. It can change lives. It can save lives.

But we must tread carefully. In a world where online harassment and cyberbullying are ever-present shadows, our digital selves can become targets. Vulnerability, while a strength in building genuine connections, can also be exploited. The anonymity of the Internet emboldens some to shed civility, to forget the human on the other side of the screen.

Boundaries become crucial. In this vast digital landscape, we must learn to erect firm boundaries around our digital selves. To decide how much we share, and with whom. Privacy settings, once an afterthought, become guardians of our online sanctity.

We navigate this digital terrain, seeking balance. Our online identity, a part of us but not the entirety. We must remember to log off. To disconnect. To sit in silence or with the chaos of the real world. Our online selves, no matter how carefully curated, cannot hug our loved ones, cannot breathe in the scent of a forest, cannot taste the salt in the sea air.

The digital self is a tool, an extension. It allows us to reach further, to learn, to grow, to connect. But it should not replace the tactile, the visceral. We are, at our core, beings of flesh and bone, of emotion and spirit. The pixels do not define us. Our actions, our kindness, our love, these are the measures of our worth.

As we continue to evolve with the digital world, let us do so with intention. Let our online identities be facets of our true selves, not replacements. Let us use the digital world to augment our reality, not escape from it.

In the end, the digital sea is vast, and we, in our digital boats, navigate its currents. Our online identities, sails in the wind. We chart our course, sometimes adrift, sometimes anchored, but always, in some way, seeking the shore. The shore of understanding, of balance, of peace.

So we log in. But we also must remember to log out. To live. To be. In the digital age, this is our challenge. This is our opportunity.

The Future of Self in the Digital Age

We're stepping into a realm where the boundaries of self are both expanding and blurring. The digital age has ushered us into a period of profound transformation. It's the skin we didn't know we could shed and grow anew.

Digital footprints trail behind us, a shadow of bytes and pixels. It's interesting, isn't it? How we exist in two realms now. Here, in the tangible, breathing world, and there, in the vast, ever-expanding digital cosmos. Our identities echo in the corridors of both, and they don't always whisper the same tales.

Consider the self as a vessel. Once, it was filled with just tangible experiences. Now, digital interactions pour in, mingling, transforming. What does it mean for the essence of who we are? The question lingers, unanswered but unavoidable.

There's a certain solitude in this digital age. The irony. We're more connected than ever, yet the intimacy of understanding oneself and being understood seems more elusive. The screens, they offer both a window and a reflection. Yet, do they mirror the truth, or just fragments of what we wish to see and be seen?

Profiles and avatars, they're facets of us, yet not the entirety. Like masks at a grand ball, they allow us to dance freely, yet at what point does the mask fuse with the skin beneath? In the digital realm, the lines between authentic self and projected self blur. We curate, consciously or not.

Interactions through screens can be both profoundly intimate and strikingly impersonal. Words typed into the void, seeking connection, seeking resonance. The digital age has redefined the way we communicate, the way we connect, and in doing so, it's redefining the self.

The echo of thoughts in silence. Ever noticed how the digital age has altered our internal monologues? The constancy of information, the barrage of the external world, it seeps into the crevices of our minds. Silence becomes a rare commodity, a treasure hunt we embark upon within the noise.

The notion of privacy morphs. Here, in this digital age, what we once held close, personal, is now currency. Shared, traded, exposed. Yet, amidst this exhibitionism and voyeurism, there's a search for genuine connection, a desire to be seen, to be recognized beyond the pixels.

Identity fluidity finds a playground in the digital world. The self is no longer static, if it ever was. We slip into different skins, explore facets of our identities with a freedom that the physical world may not offer. But in this fluidity, there's a quest for anchorage, a core that remains immutable.

Data, the digital age's currency. Our likes, dislikes, the trails we leave behind, they shape a digital self that algorithms understand, perhaps more than we understand ourselves. They predict, they categorize, they shape the experiences fed back to us. How does this feedback loop mold the self?

There's empowerment in digital anonymity and also a paradox. The freedom to express without constraint, without fear, but at what cost? When the lines blur between expression and escapism, do we risk losing a part of ourselves, or perhaps, do we find fragments we never knew existed?

The future of self in the digital age is both a promise and a conundrum. The potential for growth, for expanded empathy through global connections is immense. Yet, as we navigate this digital landscape, the compass that guides us needs recalibration. The principles, the values that anchor us.

Spirituality and mindfulness, they find a new canvas in the digital age. As we seek to understand the self, the quest turns inward with the world at our fingertips. It's a paradox, a dance of the ancient and the contemporary. How we balance this, integrate it into the essence of who we are, is the journey ahead.

The future of self is not just a reflection of how technology shapes us but how we shape it. The tools, they're neutral, extensions of our will, our desires. It's the choices we make, the awareness we bring to each click, each swipe, that will define the trajectory of self in the digital age.

As we stand at the crossroads, the digital horizon stretching before us, it's clear. The exploration of self, within and without, is an ever-evolving narrative. The digital age, with its complexities and contradictions, offers both the map and the terrain. It's a journey of discovery, of understanding, and ultimately, of integration. The future of self, it seems, is a story we're writing with every byte, every interaction, in this vast digital expanse.

Chapter 13:
Embracing the Multitude Within

As we journeyed together, unraveling the layers that compose the self, one thing became crystal clear: we are not monoliths. The multitude within each of us begs for recognition, for understanding, and, ultimately, for acceptance. To embrace this multitude is not an act of defiance against the simplicity often sought in life, but rather, it's an acknowledgment of our inherent complexity as human beings.

Understanding the self, as we've explored, is far from a straightforward process. It's a journey that meanders through the physical, mental, and spiritual landscapes that constitute our being. Each aspect of ourselves, from the neurological to the psychological, the social, and beyond, intertwines intricately, forming a mosaic that is uniquely ours. The essence of self, thus, is not found in isolation but in the confluence of these myriad streams.

Our consciousness, emerging from the depths of nothingness into the light of awareness, serves as the foundation upon which the self is built. It's in this awareness that we begin to perceive the multitude within us, navigating through our emotions, our memories, and our evolving identities. As working professionals navigating the complexities of the 21st-century world, the challenge then becomes how to balance these multiple facets while maintaining a sense of coherence and authenticity.

The brain, with its remarkable plasticity, underlies our capacity for change. It's a testament to our potential for growth and adaptation, allowing us to reinvent ourselves in response to changing circumstances. Yet, the same brain also ties us to patterns of behavior and thought, to emotions that can both illuminate and obscure our understanding of ourselves.

In examining the psychological, social, and emotional dimensions of the self, we confront the forces that shape us, from the societal to the intimately personal. Our interactions, our roles, and our relationships all act as mirrors, reflecting parts of ourselves we might not otherwise see. It's in this reflection that the opportunity for self-discovery lies, enabling us to peel away the layers of conditioning and expectation that cloud our true essence.

Our memories, those repositories of our experiences, play a pivotal role in this process. They are the narrative threads from which our identity is woven, a continuously evolving tapestry. This tapestry, with its patterns of forgetting and remembering, shapes not only who we are but also who we have the potential to become. It's a vivid reminder that the self is not static but a dynamic being, ever in flux.

Philosophically, the quest to understand the self raises existential questions that have perplexed humanity across ages and cultures. "Who am I?" is not just a question of identity but of purpose and meaning. It's a question that prompts us to look beyond the surface, to explore the spiritual dimensions that offer depth to our existence.

Spirituality, whether grounded in religious traditions or the secular practice of mindfulness, provides a lens through which the multitude within can be viewed with compassion and wisdom. It invites us to transcend the immediate, to find solace and strength in the connectedness that binds us to something greater than ourselves.

In embracing the digital age, we confront new challenges and opportunities in understanding the self. Technology, with its power to connect and isolate, to create and obscure, adds another layer to the complexity of our being. The digital self is both a reflection and a construction, a new frontier in the exploration of our identity.

The changing self, adaptable and resilient, moves through life's transitions with an innate capacity for reinvention. This capacity, however, is not infinite nor infallible. It requires nourishment, through mindfulness, reflection, and the continuous pursuit of self-awareness. It's a process that demands patience, for the journey into the self is as challenging as it is rewarding.

As working professionals, we often find ourselves ensnared in the demands of the external world, losing sight of our internal landscapes. Yet, it's in the exploration of these landscapes that we discover not just our potential for success but our capacity for fulfillment. The multitude within, with all its contradictions and complexities, holds the key to our authenticity, to a life lived with purpose and passion.

To embrace this multitude is to embark on a lifelong journey, one that requires courage, curiosity, and compassion. It's a journey that asks us to be present, to engage with the world and with ourselves in a way that is both reflective and intentional.

In the end, the multitude within is not something to be feared or suppressed but celebrated. Our flaws, our strengths, our dreams, and our fears—all contribute to the richness of our being. They are the colors with which we paint the canvas of our lives, the music to which our individual dance is choreographed.

Therefore, let us move forward with an open heart and an open mind, embracing the multitude within with kindness and understanding. For in doing so, we not only enrich our own lives but also the lives of those around us, contributing to a world that acknowledges and celebrates the complexity of the human spirit.

To conclude, embracing the multitude within is more than an act of self-discovery; it's an act of self-liberation. It frees us from the confines of a singular identity, inviting us to experience the full spectrum of our humanity. In this liberation lies our true power, the power to transform ourselves and, by extension, the world around us.

Appendix A:
Tools for Self-Discovery

Tools. They're what humans have used since the dawn of time to shape the world. But what about the tools to shape the inner world? The journey we've been on twists and turns, diving into the layers that compose the self. Now, grounded in understanding, it's time for action. Self-discovery is not just inquiry but practice. Here, we've curated tools that act as lanterns along the path inward.

Exercises for Mindfulness and Reflection

Mindfulness is the art of being here, in the now. It's simple. Not easy. Like the sky watches clouds pass, we watch thoughts. We begin.

- **Five Minutes of Breath:** Sit. Close your eyes. Breathe. Inhale. Exhale. Focus on the breath's journey. Thoughts will come. Let them pass. Return to your breath. This is your anchor.

- **The Daily Gratitude List:** Morning or evening. Take a moment. Reflect on three

151

things you are grateful for. Big. Small. It doesn't matter. Write them down. This act shifts perspectives, shines light on the unnoticed.

- **The Mirror Exercise:** Stand in front of a mirror. Look into your own eyes. Speak your name. Say, "I see you. I accept you. I love you." Awkward? Maybe. Powerful? Yes. It's about seeing. Truly seeing.

These practices are beginnings. Tools to return to, to hone, to make your own. Mindfulness isn't a destination. It's a way of being, moving through the world.

Recommended Reading

Books. They're not just pages and ink (or pixels, if you prefer). They're doors. Portals. Here are some to step through:

- **The Power of Now** - It speaks of the eternal present. The past is memory. The future, imagination. All we have is now. This book, a beacon, guides back to the present moment.

- **Siddhartha** - A journey of self-discovery, echoing our own. It's a reminder that the path inward is both universal and deeply personal.

Siddhartha's search for enlightenment mirrors the quests we embark upon.

- **Wherever You Go, There You Are** - Mindfulness. Explained, demystified. This book, a map for the modern explorer, invites to a journey within with clarity and simplicity.

Books are companions. Mentors without breath. They ask for nothing but time and offer windows into other minds, other lives, other selves.

In closing this appendix, remember: tools and exercises are just that. Tools. They require use to be of any value. The real work, the true journey, is yours and yours alone. These tools, these books—they're but signposts along the way. Where you go, how you get there, what discoveries await—that's on you.

It's a journey. It always was. There's a world within, vast and uncharted. Let's explore.

Exercises for Mindfulness and Reflection

In the blur of everyday life, moments for personal reflection are rare. They're gold. Found in early mornings or late nights. Interrupting the routine can start with simply pausing. You've paused before, on a walk or glancing out of a window. That's where mindfulness begins. It's not about silence; it's about noticing the noise and finding yourself within it. This chapter is dedicated to exercises that help bring us to such moments of clarity.

Start small. A minute can suffice. Sit and breathe. Feel the air, its temperature, its movement. Notice it filling your lungs, your chest rising, and falling. Thoughts will bombard you. That's fine. Notice them too but don't invite them to stay. Let them pass, like clouds on a windy day. That's the essence of mindfulness - observing without attachment.

Write. It's a simple action, but profound. Carry a small notebook, something that fits in the palm of your hand. Throughout the day, jot down thoughts, feelings, observations. No filter. The mundane, the profound, it all matters. It's not about the quality of writing; it's the act of noticing and noting. This exercise sharpens the mind's eye.

Walk without a destination. Let your feet decide the route. Observe the rhythm of your steps, the patterns on the sidewalk, the faces of passersby. Each step, each breath, a reminder: you're here, part of a larger whole, yet distinctly you. There's a meditation in motion, a mindfulness in acknowledging the journey, not just the destination.

Listen. Really listen. To a piece of music, to the wind, to the city's heartbeat. Close your eyes and let the sounds surround you. What do you hear that you hadn't noticed before? Sounds can tell stories, evoke memories, stir emotions. Listening, deeply, is an act of mindfulness.

Practice gratitude. Each night, list three things you're thankful for. They can be as simple as a cup of coffee that was especially satisfying or as substantial as the support of a loved one during a tough time. Gratitude shifts focus, illuminates the often overlooked positives, and cultivates a habit of noticing the good.

Eat consciously. Take a meal and really focus on it. The textures, the flavors, the smells. Eating, an act often rushed, holds layers of experience when we slow down. It's mindful eating. It brings an awareness of the body, its needs, its responses. It's gratitude, too, for the nourishment provided.

Sleep mindfulness. Before sleeping, reflect on your day. Start from waking up and recount, briefly, the day's events. Observe how recalling the day affects your body, your emotions. It's a practice in detachment and understanding, seeing the day from a distance as it were, acknowledging without judgment.

Reflection in silence. Find a spot, a sanctuary of quiet. Sit and let silence envelop you. It's uncomfortable, at first. We're conditioned to noise, to constant stimulation. Silence confronts. It allows thoughts and feelings, often ignored, to surface. It's in this space that reflection deepens, that self-awareness grows.

Connect with nature. There's mindfulness in acknowledging we're part of something larger. Stand outside, feel the sun, the breeze. Notice the intricate patterns on leaves, the vastness of the sky. Nature, in its relentless cycle, mirrors life itself. It's a reminder of renewal, growth, and the beauty of the transient.

Engage in art. Whether creating or observing, art induces mindfulness. It demands focus, evokes emotion, and stirs thought. It's a reflection of the human condition, of the textures and colors of life. Art, in its myriad forms, is a pathway to understanding oneself and the world.

Practice saying no. Mindfulness is also about setting boundaries, understanding limits. It's acknowledging that the self needs space to breathe, grow, and reflect. Saying no, thoughtfully and respectfully, is an act of self-care. It allows for the preservation of self, ensuring we're not lost in the demands of the world.

Find a mindfulness partner. This journey is deeply personal, yet shared experiences can amplify its benefits. Share insights, challenges, moments of clarity. It's not about giving advice, but about listening, understanding, and walking alongside someone on their path of self-discovery.

Dedicate yourself to a cause. Mindfulness extends beyond the self. It's recognizing our interconnectedness. Contributing to something larger, volunteering, advocating, brings a sense of purpose, of belonging. It's mindfulness in action, applying self-awareness to make a tangible difference.

Reflection and mindfulness are lifelong practices. They require consistency, patience, and kindness toward oneself. Start where you are, use what you have, do what you can. It's a journey within, to uncover, understand, and nurture the self. In doing so, we find our place in the world, our purpose, and the intricate web of connections that bind us all.

Recommended Reading

There's something about books. The way they feel in your hands. The way pages whisper as they turn. They're vessels of discovery, especially when you're on a journey inward. In the maze of self-discovery, books serve as the compass, guiding us through the layers of our mind and spirit. The following titles are curated for the explorer, the inquirer, the professional seeking understanding beyond the visible.

Some books are lighthouses in the vast sea of consciousness. They don't just illuminate paths but also reveal the hurdles, the undercurrents we might not see. One such beacon is *The Untethered Soul*, by Michael A. Singer. A profound look at the nature of self and the freedom that comes from understanding it. It teaches the art of letting go, of expanding beyond our perceived limits.

Then there's *The Power of Now*, by Eckhart Tolle. It's more than words on paper. It's an experience, a conversation that pulls you into the moment. The present. It's where the essence of self thrives, away from the echoes of the past and the whispers of the future. Tolle speaks with simplicity, yet each sentence is a doorway to depth, to understanding the self in its purest form.

In the dance of the conscious and the subconscious, *Thinking, Fast and Slow*, by Daniel Kahneman, plays a pivotal role. It's a deep dive into the pools of our thought processes and the biases that shape them. Understanding the self requires peeling back the layers of our decision-making, our beliefs. Kahneman's work is a mirror, reflecting not just who we are but how we think, decide, and act.

For those who tread the path of spirituality, *The Book of Awakening*, by Mark Nepo, is a daily companion. It's a collection of insights, a map of the spiritual journey through the year. Each page a reflection, each reflection a stepping stone to the self beyond the roles and identities we don.

And then there's exploration of the self through others' stories. *Man's Search for Meaning*, by Viktor Frankl, is a testament to the strength of the human spirit, to finding purpose amidst the bleakest landscapes. Frankl's journey through concentration camps to discovery of logotherapy shows how understanding suffering and seeking meaning are integral to understanding the self.

The metaphysical journey into the self isn't always linear, nor is it confined to the tangible. *Siddhartha*, by Hermann Hesse, is a narrative exploration, a story that parallels our own search for understanding. It's simplicity and depth. A river of self-discovery, flowing through the life of one who sought enlightenment.

On the shores of memory and identity, *The Tell-Tale Brain*, by V.S. Ramachandran, offers a glimpse into the neurological underpinnings of our sense of self. Through case studies and clear explanations, Ramachandran bridges the gap between the physical brain and the metaphysical self, revealing the intricate dance of memory, identity, and consciousness.

In the realm of emotional self-discovery, *Emotional Intelligence*, by Daniel Goleman, shines a light on understanding our emotions and their power in shaping our lives. It's not just about what we feel, but how we navigate, understand, and use those feelings. In the journey to self-understanding, acknowledging and harnessing emotions is crucial.

For a dive into the dynamics of the social self, *Quiet*, by Susan Cain, is a revelation. It's an exploration of introversion in a world that can't stop speaking. Understanding the self includes understanding how we interact with the world, how we recharge, and how we contribute. Cain's work is an affirmation of the quiet strength within many of us.

In the landscape of professional self-discovery, *Drive*, by Daniel H. Pink, is a roadmap. It outlines what truly motivates us, beyond the traditional carrots and sticks. Understanding what drives us at work is a critical component of understanding our professional self, of aligning our career with our inner values and motivations.

As we navigate identity and role playing, *The Authenticity Project*, by Clare Pooley, offers a fictional yet profound insight. Through the intertwined lives of its characters, it questions authenticity in our modern world. It makes you wonder about the masks we wear and the freedom that comes from laying them down.

Every journey has its share of forgetting and remembrance. *The Art of Memory*, by Frances A. Yates, delves into the historical techniques of memory and how they shape our understanding of the self. It's a bridge between the past and present, showing how memory constructs and deconstructs the narratives of who we are.

Finally, as we explore the philosophy of self, *The Alchemist*, by Paulo Coelho, serves as a reminder of our individual quests for meaning. It's a story, a fable, about following one's dream, understanding one's heart. In the simplicity of Santiago's journey, we find reflections of our own paths to self-discovery.

These books are tools, keys to unlocking parts of ourselves yet undiscovered. They weave through the complexities of the self, shedding light on our inner workings, our external expressions, and the myriad ways in which we navigate the world. In them, we find companionship, insight, and guidance on the ever-winding path to understanding who we are.

Acknowledgement

To my wife, Christina. I'm forever grateful for our life, our love, how we move through this world together. You are the universe. My everything. And to our daughter, Flynn Parker Rose. Thank you for reminding me everyday what it means to be present. To love with my entire self. You can be and do anything you wish my love.

Special thanks to my mother, Lesley. To my father, Steve. My siblings Derek, Zach and Adrienne. Our experiences together have led to a much deeper understanding of self.

Much gratitude to B-Love. Thank you for providing a safe space to explore the nature and structure of reality.

www.ingramcontent.com/pod-product-compliance
Lightning Source LLC
Chambersburg PA
CBHW020318290526
45785CB00007B/2831